THE LAD CALLED
RATE

Written by: Donna Gene Stankey
Co-Authored by: Ramona Hammel

Ordering Information:
You may search this book in Amazon, Barnes & Nobles and other online retailers by searching using the ISBN below.

ISBN: 978-1-958920-15-2 (Paperback)
        978-1-958920-16-9 (Ebook)

CONTENTS

CHAPTER 1

It was Sunday morning and time for the chore of driving flies out of the house. Mina hated this job, but how else was one to rid the house of flies? Seemed that July and August were the worst months, when it was hot and dry after a wet spring, and this year seemed to be a really fertile one for flies. Why, when it was going to storm, they clung to the screen door in swarms and crawled in every little crack and crevasse. Of course, every time Ralph went in and out, he let in at least a dozen it seemed. Blanche wasn't near as bad, for of course, she stayed put much longer at a time than her brother.

Miney had finished drawing all the shades in the house, and now she handed dish towels to Blanche and Millie. Blanche came from the bedroom, Millie the kitchen, while Miney took the parlor, and Ralph stood by the north dining room door ready to open the screen at his mother's command. Here they came, waving the towels, and the flies swarmed ahead of them.

"Ralph, get that door open."

"Yes, Ma."

"Now, you be ready to close it as soon as we get these flies out. We don't want them coming back in."

Ralph did as he was bidden, and when the last flies flew past, he slammed the screen door with a bang.

"Goodness, Ralph, I didn't mean for you to take the door off the hinges. There, that's done. Now, you and Blanche hurry and get ready for church. We're a little late, so don't dawdle."

Flies were just something everyone accepted as inevitable, Miney included. Neither she nor Millie stopped to consider that it was only a few yards from the back door to where they slopped the hogs, and my, how the flies did swarm about the sides of the feeding troughs, which were covered with remnants of swill and sour milk. Then, the cattle came almost to the back door to drink from the large tank by the creaking wooden windmill. Of course, not much farther away was the sheep barn, still partly full of manure because Millie had been too busy with other things to get it hauled out yet, and then there was the barnyard, which always seemed to be wet where the manure piles had stood.

The horse stable and cow stable were kept clean, but there was always a calf or two tied on the barn floor, and the litter simply built up around them. Really, a farm was a fly-breeding paradise. They had screens for some of the windows and screen doors, but nothing ever seemed to fit quite as snugly as it should, and those flies could always find a place to crawl into the house.

The first of the week, they kept busy with a flyswatter, and it wasn't so bad. However, come Sunday, the flies were pretty thick once again. It wasn't as though they were the only family with this problem because they weren't. All the neighbors had the same chore on Sunday morning, and until someone came up with a better idea of how to control the fly population, this method would suffice.

The threshing rig had come and gone, and now, there was a big bin on the south side of the granary full of dark golden kernels of wheat. Ralph had been glad to lend a hand shoveling the grain back in the bin from where the men dumped their sacks at the front. He had liked the feel of the cool grain coming up between his toes; and when he sank above his knees, he had pretended he was sinking in quicksand. He'd heard Grandfather tell about someone getting caught in quicksand, and if there hadn't been two men to help him out, the man would have died. Ralph had thought about that for days and wondered how it would feel to have his body being slowly sucked down, not being able to help himself, until his mouth and nose went beneath the surface and filled with the sodden, slimy sand.

Anyway, it had been great fun playing in the bin of wheat, so a couple of days after they had threshed, for want of something to do, he had clambered into the bin to play. Millie had found him there and had sternly told him the wheat bin was not meant for him to play in, and he had shown Rate where his antics had thrown some grain out onto the granary floor. Ralph couldn't understand why it mattered that much when they had a whole bin full, but he had not argued with his father.

The very next afternoon, he had once again been bored with life and could think of nothing to do to keep himself busy. He started thinking about how he liked the feel of the cool grain on his bare feet and legs, and before he knew it, he found himself back in the bin once more. The thought did occur to him that he would be in trouble if Pa caught him, but then, Pa had gone back to the field right after dinner, and he shouldn't be up afore suppertime. Rate was having a glorious time when he looked out the doorway—the doors had not been hung as yet—and spied his father headed his way. Cripes! He had better get out of there fast. He swung over the side of the bin, went through the door to the toolshed, ran out of the toolshed door, smack-dab into the waiting arms of his father. Rate's heart sank. Pa scowled something fierce as he held him at arm's length.

"Boy, didn't I tell you just yesterday you were not to play in that wheat bin?"

"Yessir."

"Then, I guess you'll just have to take what you got coming."

He moved off a few feet to pick a two-by-two picket from the fence around the driveway. Ralph looked at the picket with misgivings, but he said nothing. Millie gave his son a good shellacking, hard enough to turn the boy's backsides black and blue for a few days. Ralph made no outcry although a few tears slipped down his cheeks to be hastily wiped off on his shirtsleeve. This was licking number two for the growing-up years.

Millie hitched the team to the wagon, which was loaded with a few bales of hay. Horatio had asked him to bring the last of it into town. The new cutting of hay was already stacked by the barn waiting for the arrival of the hay baler.

Timothy hay to feed the nation's horses was a good money crop for farmers. All those horses stabled in the cities consumed tons of hay each year, and the farmer was the supplier. Millie always sold his crop as soon as the baler left, but he kept enough bales to furnish hay for his father's horses. The hay for his own livestock was mowed away in the barn for convenient use during the winter months. Millie only baled what he intended to sell for ready money.

He and Ralph started off at a brisk trot for Elsie; they turned east onto the Ridge Road and had just passed Sherman's when they met a man driving a pair of bays on a rather rickety-looking wagon. Ralph hadn't known the man although his father seemed to recognize the farmer since they both drew up their teams.

"Nice-lookin' team you got there," observed the man.

"Yup. They're good workers, steady and not too old either."

"How old be they?"

"Look for yourself. Make it a practice to let a man do his own looking," said Millie.

The man fastened the lines, climbed down, and proceeded to examine Millie's team. He looked at their teeth, he checked their feet and legs; in fact, very little escaped his eye. Millie sat relaxed on the wagon, seeming to pay little attention, but Ralph noted his father looked rather critically at the other man's team.

"How'd you like to make a trade, Millie?"

"Sam, you make me a good enough offer, and I just might be interested."

"Fifty dollars. I'll go fifty dollars."

"I said a good offer. You know that team of yours has at least eight years on this team. They could use a little more weight to be in fit condition. That off one has a collar sore." Millie knew he could heal this in short order with blue vitriol and rest.

"Well, maybe you're right. I'm not sayin' they be that old, mind you. Tell you what. I'll go seventy-five. Cash money. Got it right here, only we got to trade right now."

Millie seemed to ponder the situation. Rate watched with interest. He knew his father had bought this team at a sale as Millie had said "for a song," and that much sounded like a good deal to him.

Finally, Millie said, "Make that an even hundred cash, and I'll do it. You'll be getting the best of the deal, I'm thinkin', but I'll take a chance."

"Sold. Let's get 'em switched. We can change harness one at a time."

"Let's see the money first."

"I've got it all."

The farmer counted out the money, and they proceeded to change harness and teams right there in the middle of the road.

As Ralph and Millie continued on their way, Millie spoke.

"Let that be a lesson to you, boy. When you trade, always get boot money. Know someone who wants a second team who'll be glad to get this one since they don't want to pay for a prime young team. I know I'll get as much or a mite more than I gave for that other team, so I'll have made a hundred clear profit. Yessir, boy, it is always wise to trade if the boot money is good enough. 'Course it helps to have an eye for horseflesh too. Now, Pa is the one who knows horses. I'm not near as good at judgin' a horse as Pa, but I'm a sight better than John. You could give him the best team in the world, and by the end of the week, he'd have nothing but a pelt of feathers. Somehow, John always gets took." Millie chuckled.

Ralph tried to digest this scrap of advice tossed out by his father. Pa sure was some businessman. Bet not many people ever swapped horses right in the middle of the road. He'd heard his grandfather complain because his uncle John just never seemed to learn about horses. 'Course, there had been a time or two when he had seen Grandfather point out some minor flaw that his father had failed to see. He guessed there just wasn't a more astute horse trader around than his grandfather. Rate made up his mind that he would try to learn as much as he could about horses so he would be like his father and grandfather instead of like Uncle John. Golly, wait until he saw Curly Sherman and told him about this. Bet Mr. Sherman had never swapped a team like that. Ralph's pride in his father grew by leaps and bounds.

*****

Ralph had already hauled wood for the day. That was one thing in favor of hot weather, it didn't take near as much kindling for the cookstove since Ma kept only as much fire as she needed to cook the meals. If it was a baking day, it took more, but she hadn't used what he'd stacked up yesterday, so it had taken only one wagonload to finish the job.

He couldn't rightly make up his mind what he should do for the rest of the morning. Pa hadn't given him any special chores, and he was tired of playing catch with himself. He had gone to see Curly, but had been told that Curly had gone to town with his father, so Rate had sauntered back home. Since Blanche had stayed over to Grandmother's yesterday, he couldn't tease her.

He ambled toward the granary where Pa had been doing some painting. Since they had just finished building the granary, Pa was in a hurry to get the new wood painted before we started getting fall rain, he'd said. Yup, there was Pa, bent over stirring a big, five-gallon pail of red barn paint. Rate watched him a moment, noticing just how enticing Millie's backsides looked where the overalls stretched tightly over his buttocks. Rate picked a picket out of the fence, moved nearer his father with careful steps, then whack! Ralph hit Millie a resounding blow, square on his posterior end. Rate laughed as Millie jumped, then realized he had better make tracks.

Out around the granary he went, by the sheep shed, and down the lane. Now, Millie was just a mite slow to follow since he took the time to pick up a gallon pail of paint and a brush; then, Millie, paint pail in one hand and brush in the other, took off after his son. Some of the paint spilled a little and splashed on his striped overalls, but Millie didn't seem to notice. He was intent on the small figure scurrying along in front of him.

Rate must have known that even with a sizable head start, his father could surely outrun him. However, he kept going as fast as his legs would carry him. They were almost to the bridge when Millie caught up with his son. Since he had transferred the brush to his left hand, he grabbed Ralph's arm with his strong right hand, lifted the boy off the ground, and plunked him down on the top rail of the lane fence. He spoke not a word, chuckled to himself, and proceeded to paint Rate's bare legs and feet bright red. One thing about Millie, he never did half a job on anything, so when he finished, Ralph was red from knee to toe, with no patch of white skin showing any place. With still no word to the boy, Millie sauntered off as if this was the most usual thing in the world— painting a small boy who hadn't dared wiggle.

Ralph sat a few moments on the fence looking at what a sight he was. He felt like crying. How was he ever to get that paint off? He knew Ma would holler at him even if it wasn't all his fault. She would likely switch his legs good since Ma sure did cotton to switching as a way of punishment. It's a wonder she hadn't killed that poor little tree south of the house, she'd broken that many switches off it. 'Course she would jaw at Pa too, not that it would do any good.

He started back for the buildings, the fine black dust from the lane sticking to the wet paint, making his legs and feet a dirty, grimy mess. Luckily he hadn't got any on his pants. Why, when Pa had started, he'd wondered if Pa was ever going to quit. He could just picture being red from head to toe, so he'd been mighty thankful when Pa had stopped.

As he came around the corner of the sheep shed, the hired man, old Charley Dodge, who had been in the Civil War, spied the boy.

"What happened to you, Rate? Did you turn Indian?" He laughed.

"Naw. I just couldn't outrun Pa, that's all. Someday I'll get even." He took a huge burdock leaf and scrubbed down the side of his leg. It came away tinged with red, but had actually made little difference to his leg. Then, he took a handful of sand and scrubbed it along his leg with the same result. The paint clung tenaciously to his skin. "Ma's going to yell something fierce if I don't get this off," he commented with a worried frown.

"Got any old gunnysacks around?"

"I guess so. Why?"

"You jest go fetch one, and we'll see what can be done 'bout that there paint."

Ralph soon returned with a torn gunnysack and watched as Charley wet a large corner of it with turpentine.

"Now, Rate, you scrub yourself good. When you've got the paint off the best you kin, use some of your ma's soap and lather up good with warm water from the reservoir. Think that'll git most of it. Now, git busy afore it gits any drier."

Ralph set to work with a will. That paint sure did stick something awful. He scrubbed with the turpentine until he felt as though the skin would come off along with the paint. He supposed Ma would be in the kitchen, so's he wouldn't stand a chance to sneak a washdish of water without her knowing it. Well, maybe if he got the most of it off, she wouldn't holler at him. After all, it was Pa's idea. He certainly never dreamed Pa would do such a thing, but one never could outguess Pa. Too bad he hadn't been able to outrun him, but then, there'd be another day.

*****

Hay baling time was always a time for an extra hand around, so Millie hired Jim Keenan. Usually Jim only worked for him by the day and always spent his nights elsewhere. This time, Jim moved into the small upstairs bedroom with Ralph being shuffled downstairs to the front bedroom.

The first morning when Miney went up to make Jim's bed, she let out an exclamation of disgust.

"Bedbug! A bedbug in this bed."

The bedding flew as she hastily gathered up the sheets, pillowcase, and light quilt. Downstairs she went and onto the porch. She stalked back upstairs, grabbed Jim's battered old valise, a pair of pants and shirt from off the chair, then down the stairs once more. Clothes and valise all went into the yard. Next, she hauled the cornhusk mattress down the stairs and out into the hot sunlight.

When Millie and Jim came up for dinner, they found the bedclothes soaking in a tub of hot water, Jim's clothes in the yard, and an extremely determined woman barring their entrance to the house.

"Jim Keenan, I found a bedbug where you slept last night, so your belongings are over there. I've gone all over that room with kerosene in hopes if there was more than one, I got them. Oh, Millie, just imagine. Bedbugs in our house."

"I'm sorry, Miney," said Jim. "But what harm's a little old bedbug?" he teased.

"Sorry! Well, you should be. Look at all the work you've caused me. There's no sense for anyone to be so dirty as to have bedbugs, Jim Keenan. I certainly am not going to have a house full of bedbugs from having you here. From now on, you can just sleep in the granary."

"The granary? Aw, Miney, ain'tcha got no heart?"

"None at all. Granary, that's where. There's an old bed in the upstairs that you and Millie can set up, and you can sleep there. I'll not have you bringing any more bedbugs into my house. Now, you hurry and get washed since I've got dinner ready to set on the table."

Jim shook his head good-naturedly as Mina went back into the house slamming the door as if to punctuate her words.

Millie and Jim moved over to the washbasin sitting on a bench by the pump to the cistern at the southeast side of the porch. Most families had a rain barrel to catch their soft water, but Horatio had put an underground cistern to the east end of the porch, which caught the rainwater coming off the eaves. During the warm months, the men always washed up there instead of in the house.

For a week after this incident, Miney checked the bedroom each day. The second day, she found another lone bug so repeated the kerosene treatment and continued to air the mattress. Since no more bugs were found, after the smell of the kerosene left, Ralph returned to the upstairs bedroom while Jim spent his nights on the second floor of the granary; it mattered not in the least to him since all he asked for was a roof over his head, good meals—and Miney certainly provided those—and a few dollars' pay each month.

Rate kept watching up the road in expectation. Last night, he had heard Pa tell Ma that the baler would be here tomorrow, and she would have some extra hands to feed. Rate had seen them bale hay before, yet he was always fascinated by the process much the same as he was fascinated by the threshing rig.

Yup. Here it came. He knew better than to get around in the way. Pa was just not one to fool around when it came time to get work done. He kept his distance as the machine came into the drive and set up between the two large stacks of hay east of the barn by the north driveway. The scales set to the south of the drive and would be used today although the baler carried its own set of scales for when they set up in a field where there were no scales available. Such would be the case when they moved to the north eighty from here.

Now that they were ready to go, Ralph came over to watch. Six horses were harnessed in place to walk steadily in a circle, round and round, turning the driveshaft, which set the baler in motion. A man methodically pitched forkfuls and shouted "Bale!" when he had thrown in enough hay for one bale. Another man put in a divider so the second bale was begun. Two men, one on each side of the machine, sat there to punch the wire into a hole where it came through and was used to tie the bale. The wire-tied bales were huge. As they came from the chute of the machine, two men dragged them to the scales where they were weighed, the weight recorded on a split four-by-four wooden tag, and the tag inserted under the wire to be held firmly in place. These bales averaged three hundred pounds each, so they were not something one man could toss around. The elevator paid for the hay by the ton as well as the fee for the baler, but each bale had to be weighed because some townspeople bought only a few bales at a time from the feedstores. The bales were immediately loaded on wagons, so Jim Keenan and Jake Finch could haul them directly to town.

Baling time was worse than threshing time as far as Miney's work was concerned. The five men who arrived with the baler would stay right here until the baling was completed, usually in four or five days. Millie might have to provide stable space and feed for six horses, but the man who owned the baler saw to taking care of them.

The men slept in the barn, so they were there for breakfast, dinner, and supper, along with Millie and Jim. Now cooking for seven hungry men for breakfast was no small task. For dinner and supper, it made nine extra since two more men came in to handle the bales from baler to scales, along with Jake. Seemed as though it took forever to do the dishes even if Blanche was there to help.

One thing was certain, they didn't get a lot of variety. Breakfast was fried eggs, fried bread, and coffee. Dinner was plenty of boiled potatoes, some sort of meat and gravy, creamed string beans from the garden or perhaps some lettuce with vinegar and sugar, bread and butter, coffee and pie. Supper consisted of the leftover potatoes cut up with leftover meat diced into them for hash, some sort of cooked vegetable, bread and butter, perhaps some canned fruit, cake, and coffee. The men didn't care all that much about variety— they wanted plain food and plenty of it. Bread, meat, and potatoes were what they appreciated most. The other things were just extra trimmings, which placed Miney a little above the average cook.

Although Mina was frugal in many ways, she always set a good table for hardworking men. It always pleased her when some of the men would take the time to tell her how good the meal was. Seemed like it made the effort more worthwhile. After all, she did get completely worn-out having to feed so many extra hands for so many days. However, it was just one more task with which a farmwife had to contend.

Rate had seen fit to ask his father if he might ride with one of the men into town, so when Jim left with the first load, Ralph went along. He liked sitting up on the bales. They smelled good. He guessed he still liked the smell of freshly mowed hay the best. Why, when they had first finished haying, he had teased to sleep out in the barn. Ma had been quick to say no, but Pa seemed to understand boys better, so he'd said, "Miney, let the boy go. I've slept in a hayloft afore this, and I can't rightly see where it hurt me." Ma had sighed and said, "Well, if your father says so, I guess it has to be all right." Yup, there were times when Pa was a lot more likely to let him do what he wanted. He guessed women were just natural-born worriers.

It had been one of those extremely hot August days, the sky a cloudless blue, and hardly a breath of air stirred the leaves on the trees; all had been quiet except for the droning of a few insects, when Rate came bursting into the house where Mina sat with some patching.

"Ma, one of Pa's old sows is in the cornfield. I tried to git her out, but she won't even budge for me." Now, the field south of the house was planted to corn, and a good-looking piece it was. "Where's Pa?" he added.

"Lawsy, Ralph, I don't hardly expect your pa till near suppertime. What shall we do? That sow will kill herself eating green corn, not to mention the havoc she'll wreak knocking it down. My oh my." Mina headed for the door to survey the scene. "Ralph, where's Grip? Maybe he'd get her out. Grip," she called. "Here, Grip."

In a few moments, the dog sauntered around the corner of the house clearly wondering what anyone wanted with him on such a hot afternoon.

"Ralph, now you take him with you into the cornfield so's he can see the sow, and then tell him to get her. If we're lucky, maybe he can get her out of there. Do you know where she got out?"

"Yup. There's a hole in the fence over yonder where a rail is busted."

"Well, she ought to remember where she got in there, I expect. See what you can do."

Ralph and the dog went down the fenceline to the hole where both of them crawled into the field.

"C'mon, Grip, I can hear that old sow over this way."

The dog followed the boy willingly, and sure enough, there was the hog gorging herself on the corn and knocking down twice as much as she could eat. Pa sure was gonna be mad over this.

"See her, Grip. Fetch, boy, fetch."

The dog perked up his ears, looked expectantly at the boy, then at the sow, but made no move.

"Fetch her, Grip. See that there hog. Now, she's got to be got outta here. Like this, see?"

The boy started to run in the direction of the hog. She raised her head while chewing noisily on the cob of corn protruding from her mouth; then, she noticed the dog, turned, and ambled off at a slow walk. Now, Grip seemed to get the idea because he barked and started in her direction.

"Good boy, Grip. Take her outta here."

The dog barked again, and the sow took off on the run. Rate watched dog and hog disappear down a row of corn and then became aware that his mother was calling him to get back to the house. Boy, old Grip sure was makin' that sow move. He just wondered how much more of Pa's corn they was knocking down.

There went that danged sow right by the hole she had come through, and she acted like she'd never seen it before. Ma was worrying now as the sow passed it for the second time. Who'd a thought she'd be so dumb 'specially with ole Grip right after her. He'd bite, she'd squeal, and then, off they'd go for another circle through the corn. Finally, they were out of sight for a long time. Then, here come that old sow right up to the fence where they was standing, and she dropped right there, pantin' somethin' fierce. Grip didn't look as if he was any too anxious to run anymore either. He tried to worry her with a few half-hearted barks, but that old sow just lay there panting.

"Grip. Grip. That's enough," cried Miney. "Oh, my, that poor thing is like to die of heat prostration. Oh dear, whatever shall I do? I know, I'll get a pail of water to help cool her off."

Mina hurried through the house to the well and in a few minutes returned with a pail brimful of cold well water. She carried the pail over to the fence where she sloshed it through the rails all over that heaving hog. Ralph watched in awe as the sow shuddered convulsively, stiffened her legs, and then went limp.

"Ma, what's wrong? She don't act right. Whyn't she get up when you doused her?"

"I-I-I don't know. She looks dreadful strange. She's not panting anymore."

"Is she...is she even breathin'?"

"Goodness, I think so. I hope so."

"Her sides aren't moving like they was," Rate observed.

Just then Grip moved closer, took a nip at a leg, and the sow didn't move; he moved up to grab an ear, and the sow didn't move. Rate reached through the fence and lifted a leg, let go, and watched it drop limply back into place.

"Oh, no," exclaimed Miney. "Ralph, I think she's dead. Whatever will your pa say?"

"What'll I say about what?" asked Millie from the door of the house, having returned sooner than Miney expected.

"Millie, I-I guess I killed one of your sows," started Mina, and then she began to cry.

Upon being questioned, Ralph related the incident to his father, who patted Miney on the shoulder and said, "Never mind,

Miney. What's done is done. I'll get her buried whilst you're getting supper. She'll bloat dreadful fast in this hot weather, so the sooner it's done, the better."

Rate would've liked to have asked Pa why the sow had died, but he sensed this was not the time to ask his father questions. The ground was hard and dry, and the sweat ran off Millie's face in rivulets as he worked diligently. Rate watched the entire proceedings with interest. The thought crossed his mind that Pa was burying an awful lot of good meat, or so it seemed to him, but he supposed Pa knew what he was doing. Still, it did seem odd that they didn't dress her out—must be something with the way she died. Maybe he'd understand better when he was older.

September soon rolled around, and Ralph was to start school this year. The night before school started, Millie called Ralph over to stand in front of him and told his son that if the teacher ever found it necessary to give him a whipping at school, he could be mighty certain he'd get the second one when he got home. Ralph looked at his father's stern face and knew that Millie meant exactly what he said. Gripes. That meant he had better be pretty darned careful for when Pa whipped, he sure didn't spare the rod. What made Pa think he'd get whipped at school anyway? He was lookin' forward to learning, and he guessed he knew how to behave.

The schoolmistress at Stafford was Miss Edah Silvernail. When Blanche first met her, the girl had been hard put not to snicker because Edah reminded her of a bird sitting on a fence since her dress was much longer in the back than in front, so it looked like tailfeathers. Besides, she was slender to the point of being skinny, and her features were rather rough-cut.

Although Blanche still stayed in Elsie with either Grandfather and Grandmother Setterington or Grandma Smith to attend the village school, no such suggestion had been made for Ralph. Of course, he was expected to walk the mile and a half regardless of the weather, for after all, he was a boy; since Blanche was a girl, this was too much to expect of her. However, Salina Clark up on the Ridge seemed to do it without any trouble. If Ralph thought anyone was showing partiality, he made no comment, nor did he hold it against his sister. In fact, he guessed he wouldn't have wanted to go to Elsie to school since his friends were neighbors. He and Don Sherman got on right fine even if Burl, who was a year younger, was always in the way. Naw, he guessed he was plenty satisfied with things just the way they was.

School wasn't half bad either. Ma had taught him some of his letters, so he had a head start on some of the others. He could count and write his numbers to ten too. While he liked learning to cipher, it was reading that interested him most. He had always wondered just how growed folks knew how to put letters together to make words; he'd often looked at books, studying the words carefully, trying to make out what they meant. It was always nice when Ma had time to read to him, but now, he was learning to read all by himself. Someday he'd be able to read growed-up books, and he could hardly wait for that time to come.

Dinner was almost finished, and while Rate felt almost full, those small boiled onions with white sauce sure had tasted good.

"Ma, is there any more onions left?"

"Well, there's a few." She scraped the dish. "There's more than I thought. How many do you want?"

"All of them. They sure tasted good," he said, smacking his lips.

"Oh, Ralph, I don't know. There's more than you'll likely want. Besides, maybe your pa would like some more."

"I'll eat them, honest, I will. I want another big dish just like I had in the first place."

"Let the boy have them," said Millie as Miney looked at him undecidedly.

"Well, all right, but be sure your eyes aren't bigger than your stomach," said Miney as she emptied the bowl into his dish.

Ralph started eating with a vim, but about halfway through, he slowed down, another mouthful, and he stopped altogether. After sitting a moment contemplating the situation, he finally said, "Ma, I'm full. Do I have to finish these?"

Millie, who had been watching his son, fully realized Ralph was already stuffed, and yet, he had to learn, so Millie said quietly, "Boy, eat your onions."

With a sidelong glance at his father, Rate dug in. He cleaned his dish just as his father said. However, he had also learned his lesson well. Never again was he to ask for seconds when he was already rather full no matter how good something tasted.

*****

Ralph tried to sneak quietly into the house and place his round tin dinner pail on the kitchen cabinet without being seen. Luck was not with him today. Just as he had carefully set the dinner pail down without so much as a tiny clatter, he turned to see his mother watching him from the dining room doorway.

"Ralph, what have you been up to now?"

"Nuthin', Ma. I just got home from school."

"I can see that. Little late, aren't you? Where'd you get the grime on your face, and look at your clothes. Ralph, did you get into a fight?"

"Well, sorta."

"What do you mean sort of? Either you got into a fight or you didn't."

Rate heaved a sigh. "I got into a fight," he admitted.

"With whom?"

"Aw, that Naegle kid. He was bragging because he can run faster than I can and was calling me turtle, so I pasted him one. Then, he hit me back, and afore I knowed it, we was on the ground. I was gettin' the best of him when Miss Silvernail came out and hauled us apart. Then, she made us stay after school awhile."

Millie had happened in as his son was describing the fight.

"See, Millie," accused Miney, "he's just a chip off the old block. Your mother tells how you and John always fought. I don't want my son to be such a ruffian."

"Boys will be boys, Miney, lessen you want him to grow up to be a sissy. Don't appear that he came out too bad. Leastways he doesn't have a black eye. Don't look like he had a bloody nose either. What more can you ask?"

"Men! I'll never understand one if I live to be a hundred."

With that, Miney pushed past Ralph to return to the dining room. She muttered to herself as she went, "Why do fists always have to settle an argument? Why can't they be more civilized? Didn't Christ teach us to turn the other cheek? Sometimes, I don't think Millie ever got past the Old Testament."

Millie winked at his son, the crinkles around his eyes deep-set with merriment.

"Well, boy, did you learn anything today?"

"Sure did, Pa. It's better not to get knocked down, but if you're down, it's a lot better bein' on top."

Millie laughed heartily.

"Rate, just remember, if you can't avoid a fight, be sure and get in the first lick. Don't never back away from a fight, but don't go around askin' for one either, and don't pick on those smaller than yourself. I won't tolerate a bully."

"Oh, no, Pa. I'd never do that. 'Course, right now at school, I'm about the smallest one. Next year, I'll be bigger than any old first grader though."

Millie chuckled at this logic. He left the kitchen while Ralph raided the cookie tin. Gosh, for a minute he had thought Pa might be mad, but he guessed Pa remembered what it was like to be a young boy. Ma sure had been upset. Guess he'd better get his face and hands washed before she yelled at him again. Then, he'd get right to his chores, and maybe by suppertime, she'd feel in a more congenial mood.

*****

Ralph peered cautiously in the kitchen door. No sign of Ma anywhere, so he slipped quietly into the house. With him, he had a green tree branch a little over two feet long that had one end sharpened to a point. He stepped noiselessly up to the cookstove, but try as he might, the lid clattered a little as he lifted it off. Darn! Oh well, no time to worry now.

He had no more than stuck the end of the stick into the coals of the nearly burned-out fire when a voice hissed, "What do you think you're doing? I'm going to tell Ma."

Rate jumped, then gained perfect aplomb and answered rather nonchalantly, "Go ahead. See if I care."

"You know Ma doesn't want you messing around in her kitchen. What are you doing anyway?" Blanche added, her curiosity showing.

"Nothing a girl would understand."

"I would so. Why are you burning that old stick?"

"Keep your mouth shut and your eyes open, and you'll find out."

"Now, you sound just like Pa."

The end of the branch had burned just a little. Ralph surveyed it critically, decided it would do, replaced the stove lid, then spoke to his sister.

"If you want to see, you'll have to follow me."

"Oh, all right. If you aren't going too far. I might still tell Ma," she threatened.

"Then, I won't show you."

Whistling somewhat tunelessly, he moved out the door.

In spite of herself, Blanche found herself following him out to the orchard where there were a goodly number of green apples on the ground. She watched as Rate stuck an apple on the end of the stick, whipped it through the air, and sent the apple flying.

"Is that all? It certainly doesn't take much to amuse a boy."

With that observation, she returned to the house.

Girls sure were silly. Well, he hadn't really expected her to be overly enthused about his game, but it was fun whether she thought so or not.

He could really whip an apple a considerable distance, and the more he practiced, the more accurate he got.

Girls just never understood anything that wasn't connected with cooking, sewing, or fancy work. Now, he couldn't understand sitting for an hour or so embroidering on some dresser scarf. 'Course, it had been kinda funny when Blanche was first learning. He remembered how Ma had said Blanche's fingers were all thumbs, and Blanche had pricked her finger; and while it bled, she cried. Still, Ma had been awful patient with her. She showed her and showed her, and when Blanche's thread got all knotted and tangled, Ma had just laughed and commented that she didn't see how a body could make such a mess out of something.

Blanche hadn't given up at all. She'd just kept right at it, and if Ma took out some of her stitches, she just put them right back in, and it wasn't long before Ma was telling her what a good job she was doing. Ma, being a perfectionist, wasn't one to give praise unless it was due either.

That was one thing about Blanche, she just never admitted she couldn't do something. He guessed Ma was right when she accused her of being an awful lot like Grandfather.

Ralph, Blanche, and Miney sat in church with Horatio and Lovina in what was known as the Setterington pew. The pew was located to the right side of the podium and resembled a box at the opera since it was cushioned in a rich dark velour and was the only one so extravagantly covered in the church. Rate wiggled a little as the minister started giving his sermon. He guessed he liked having the cushions to sit on since they were a lot more comfortable than those hard wooden seats. Ma always scowled fiercely if he wiggled during the sermon. Sometimes, if Blanche sat by him, she'd pinch him and make him squirm. While he daren't do anything back right then, he had his ways of getting even. He never tattled on his sister, he just used his own methods of retaliation.

The minister was really getting all het up today since his topic was "the wages of sin is death." Rate didn't quite understand what was being said, but Grandfather kept nodding his head and saying "Amen," so he guessed Grandfather agreed with what the preacher said. He'd asked Ma 'bout it one day, why Grandfather often did this, and Ma had said it was to show that he agreed.

Grandmother didn't say anything, simply sat there poker-faced and only nodded her head.

Sometimes, Grandfather acted as though the preacher was talking just to him, and Rate wondered if he would ever get big enough to understand what was being said. Right now, all he knew was that if one wanted to have eternal life, a life after death, which he supposed meant going to heaven, he sure as heck didn't want to sin. He supposed those people who drank in the saloons were sinners, and he knew that it was sinful to lie or cheat or steal, but he wasn't sure if this covered everything or not.

He wondered if card-playing was sinful. He was mindful of hearing Ma tell how when Blanche was little she'd really embarrassed Ma something awful. This had happened before he was even born. It seemed that Blanche and Mina had gone over to Grandfather's after church. Well, Blanche had one of those little cards they often got in Sunday school, and she had gone up to Grandfather and asked, "Grandfather, is this a pedlow card?"

Grandfather had then asked, "Blanche, do your parents use pedro cards?"

Blanche had answered honestly, "They plays with cards."

Miney had just entered the room in time to hear Grandfather say, "Blanche, your parents should not be playing cards of any sort."

"Father Setterington," interrupted Miney, "if you want to know whether Millie and I play cards, why don't you ask one of us? It is not right for you to question Blanche since she is only a child."

"All right, Mina. I will ask it of you. Do you and Milt play cards?" asked Horatio, his black eyes boring into the fierce blue eyes of his daughter-in-law.

Miney held her head a bit higher and said, "Yes, on occasion we do play cards. At Grange meetings they usually play after the business meeting." It wasn't often Miney felt this brave around her father-in-law.

Horatio had stared at her a moment while Miney struggled not to let her eyes waver and fall. Just this once she would stand up to him. She found it easier since Lovina was not in the room.

Finally, Horatio had spoken although not unkindly.

"Cards are the devil's advocate, Miney, take my word for it. Most things start small, but that's all the foothold the devil needs. I hope in the future you and Milt will find it in your heart to refuse temptation. Remember 'Get thee behind me, Satan,' and do just that. A person must be strong to withstand the temptations of the devil."

Well, what else was Ma to do? She half promised Grandfather that she wouldn't play cards again. Must be card-playing was a sin, or Grandfather wouldn't have been so insistent on the matter. Rate knew that he'd never seen his folks play, although at Grange meetings at neighbors' houses, the menfolk often played and occasionally some of the women. It had looked like a lot of fun to him, and he wasn't sure just where the devil fitted in. Guess he'd understand when he was older.

While he had been pondering the situation, the sermon ended, and everyone rose to sing the closing hymn. When he slid out of his seat, he stepped on Blanche's foot knowing she couldn't do a thing about it without drawing Ma's attention. The hymn was "Rock of Ages," and Ralph raised his voice in song, his face a picture of innocence.

CHAPTER 2

Birthday time for Ralph rolled around, and he hadn't forgotten what Blanche had had for her present, so he waited like a babe in a nettle patch, hoping that Millie would ask him what he wanted for his present. Two days before the eventful day, Millie spoke to his young son.

"Rate, what's the day after tomorrow?"

"Saturday."

"Is that all?"

"It's my birthday too," he ventured.

"Is it now? And what would you be liking for a present this year?"

"Bananas," Ralph almost shouted.

"Bananas! Whatever for?" Millie laughed.

"To eat. Blanche got her oranges, and I'd like bananas. They's the best eating of anything. Can I have them, Pa?"

"We'll see. Can't tell you for sure and spoil the surprise, now can I? I'd thought maybe you'd like a new slingshot or something, but no, you want bananas because Blanche had oranges."

"Not because Blanche had oranges, but because I like bananas," he clarified.

"Well, have it your way."

The morning of Ralph's birthday dawned crisp and cold even though the sun shone pleasantly enough. Ralph wanted to ask his father whether he had decided on his birthday present, but he daren't. All he could do was keep busy and hope Pa would go to town after dinner. Pa and Ma had bought groceries yesterday when they went to bring Blanche home from Grandma Smith's. He knew of no reason for his father to go to town again. Rate got around and hauled wood right after breakfast while Millie was in the barn cleaning stables and doing the rest of the chores. Ralph was on tenterhooks waiting to see what his father intended. The thought crossed his mind that perhaps they had bought some small article for him yesterday.

Shortly after dinner, Millie left for town. Not a word had he said to Ralph before he left, and if he noticed that the boy hadn't eaten a very big dinner, he didn't say anything.

"Why do you keep watching out the window? Bet I know. You think Pa's going to bring you some old bananas just because he brought me oranges."

"Well, he didn't say he wouldn't," countered Ralph.

"Didn't say he would either," jeered Blanche. "What makes you think he'll spend all that money on you? Bananas are frightfully expensive, I heard Ma say so."

"I dunno. Pa just might."

"When he doesn't, just remember I told you so."

Perhaps Blanche was right. Pa never had said he'd get them, but the fact of the matter was, Pa hadn't said he wouldn't. At least Rate could still hope, even if Blanche had thrown a wet towel on his thoughts.

It was late in the afternoon when Millie and the cutter turned into the yard; already dusk had fallen, and crane his neck as he might, Ralph could get no hint of anything Pa had with him. He never gave a thought to the weather being only about fifteen degrees above zero, so if Millie did have fruit in the cutter, it most certainly would be covered with the horsehide robe. He watched apprehensively as his father drew the team up as they reached the house.

"Rate! Well, boy, where are you?" bellowed Millie.

"Here I am, Pa. What do you want?" Rate called from the doorway.

"Just wondered if you was about."

Millie climbed out of the cutter and reached back for something. As he turned around, Ralph's eyes nearly popped out of his head.

"Pa," he said in awe. "You did it. You brought me bananas. Oh, Pa."

"Don't just stand there, boy. Let me in the house so's I can set them down."

Ralph eyed his father in wonder. Millie had not bothered with a measly few bananas, oh, no, he had brought home a whole stalk of them.

"Well, Rate, you just gonna stand there looking?" Millie laughed as he stood the stalk against the wall.

"Do I get to eat all I want?"

"They're all yours, so I reckon so."

"Millie, he'll get sick," put in Mina.

"That's what you said about Blanche and the oranges, and she never got sick, now did she?"

"No, but you know how Ralph likes bananas. What if he doesn't know when to stop?"

"Then he'll get a bellyache. Miney, just keep still and let the boy be."

Ralph was still gazing at the bananas. Why, there must be more'n a hundred. Well, maybe not that many, but my, there was an awful lot of them.

"Ma, can I start eating?"

"Your father says so. Just you mind you don't get sick to your stomach, and don't try to hog them down. No one is going to take them away from you."

"I won't. Here, Ma, don't you want one?" Ralph broke off the first banana and offered it to his mother.

"Thank you, Ralph, but you had better have the first one."

"But I want you to have one, and Pa, and here, Blanche, don't you want one?"

"I guess maybe I will. I think Pa got you more bananas than he got me oranges."

"What did you expect, Blanche, a whole tree?" Millie chuckled.

"Of course not," she snapped. Then, she added in a more modulated tone, "Well, maybe it just seems like more." She took the proffered banana somewhat hesitatingly, wanting it…and yet not wanting it.

Goodness. Now, who'd have thought Pa would have bought all those bananas for Ralph? Bet they cost more than the oranges. Somehow, she just hadn't thought Pa would be that foolish. Ralph sure was going to act smart just because he got what he wanted for once. Oh, well, at least he wasn't selfish and had wanted to share with everyone. Sometimes, Pa was just hard to figure out. There were times when he acted as though Ralph was really the cat's meow, yet, when it really counted, she knew she always came out best.

Pa never said anything to her if she shirked her work, yet he never let Ralph get by without doing his. 'Course, part of this was because she was Ma's favorite, no doubt about that, and that was just because she had had the good fortune to be born a girl. Grandma Smith had told her that one day when she had been lording it over Ralph, and Grandma had peered at her through those steel-rimmed glasses, and the tone of her voice had made Blanche just a little ashamed of herself for teasing her brother. After all, she was more fortunate because Ma and even Pa most always favored her, and it really wasn't very nice of her to throw it up to Ralph. He couldn't help it because he was born a boy, but somehow, she didn't think Ralph would have liked being a girl even if he could have had a choice. Nope, she was sure he was entirely satisfied being a boy.

*****

Ralph had been standing by the window watching the huge flakes of snow drift lazily to the ground. It was pretty when it came down like this, and besides, there wasn't much else to do at Grandmother's except be quiet and not bother the grownups that is. As he stood there, he absentmindedly kept wiggling a tooth that was getting mighty loose and near the dropping-out stage.

"Rate, what are you doing?"

"Just looking out the window, Grandfather."

"No, I mean what's that you've got in your mouth?"

"Oh. A loose tooth. See?" He opened his mouth to display a slightly askew tooth.

"Come here, boy. I can't see it from clear over there."

"Uh-uh. If I do, you'll pull it."

"Now, what would I pull it for?" Rate eyed him suspiciously, mulling over in his mind his grandfather's question. "Well, Rate, what's taking so long?"

The boy finally edged over to his grandfather and stood in front of him with a somewhat wary look.

"Open up and let's see that tooth." Rate obediently opened his mouth, and Horatio peered at the small baby teeth. "Is this the one?" he asked as he tentatively touched the wobbly tooth.

"Uh-huh," acknowledged Ralph with his mouth still open.

Just then, Horatio gave a little shove with his finger, and Ralph hollered. "You pulled it, just like I knowed you would. You pulled my tooth," was the indignant accusation.

"No, boy, I simply pushed it out. There's a difference." Horatio chuckled. "Now, doesn't that feel better already?"

The boy was angry, and he scowled his displeasure, but he dared not view his thoughts aloud. He felt his grandfather had tricked him, and it hurt his manly pride. Horatio sensed the lad's struggle to keep to himself the thoughts that were churning inside. To make amends, he gave the boy a silver dollar telling him that that was a pretty good price for a worn- out tooth. Rate thanked him for the money, while underneath he still seethed. Next time, he'd know better, and he'd listen more carefully to how Grandfather worded what he said.

Usually, the only gift Blanche had for her mother at Christmas was one she had made at school or something Pa had bought to come from all three of them. This year was going to be different. Several weeks ago, she had noticed an advertisement on a soap wrapper at Grandmother's that for ten soap wrappers and fifteen cents, she could get a sugar spoon. She had asked some of her girlfriends about wrappers, and in a few weeks, she had had the necessary amount of wrappers as well as the money. Then, she had waited impatiently for the package to come in the mail; she had had it sent to her in care of Grandmother so there would be no chance of her mother opening the package by mistake.

When it finally arrived, Blanche was delighted. The small fluted bowl of the spoon was gold in color while the handle was silver; Blanche thought it was beautiful and could hardly wait until the day of gift-giving arrived.

To say that Miney was surprised at Blanche's gift would indeed be an understatement. She was almost as delighted as the young girl. It was certainly a gift she would treasure all her life. It graced Miney's table every day, and Blanche was truly proud of her accomplishment.

Rate too was pleased with Christmas. Ma and Pa had bought him a new slate to take the place of the old one, which had been Ma's and had a crack diagonally across it, making it difficult to use. The new one had four usable sides; it was like having two small slates, but they were hinged together so they could be folded for storage in the desk or spread out for use. Of course, a body didn't have to spread them out; they could be kept folded and written on both sides, or they could be turned to bring the used sides together, and the clean sides were then ready to be written on. Rate was sure his was quite the nicest slate anyone had in school.

*****

Millie had finished cleaning the cow stables and had put the cows back in the barn. He stood for a moment watching them eagerly eat the fresh hay he had just forked into their mangers, the wooden stanchions creaking in protest as the cows strained against them to reach what looked to be a choice morsel the farthest from their reach. Well, that was done, and there'd be nothing more to do today until time for chores at night.

He was in hopes Cash Waldron would be over in the afternoon for a game of checkers. Somehow, he and Cash never did seem to get tired of checker playing. Sometimes, Miney asked him how they could get any pleasure from it when they'd sit for hours at a time, hunched over the checkerboard on their knees, neither speaking, intent upon the moves to be made. Wasn't that just like a woman? 'Course a woman would never be able to keep her mouth shut for that long a time. Many's the time when Miney got to rambling on, he felt he just had to shut her up, so he'd say, "Miney, keep still." He knew it hurt her feelings, but her chattering just rankled sometimes. Now, he and Cash did their talking at other times; during a game was no time to let senseless talking divert their concentration.

As Millie came by the horse stable, he heard Rate's voice yelling, "Get off my foot, Mage. Get off my foot."

He stepped through the doorway into the stable, and there was Ralph, standing in the stall alongside Mage, whacking the large bay horse with his felt hat, yelling at the horse who stood very unconcerned, not moving a muscle.

"What's all the screeching about?" asked Millie suppressing a laugh.

"Pa," came the relieved reply. "I can't get Mage to move off my foot. I can't pull it out either. He just won't move no matter how I hit and shove."

"Rate, use your head for something besides a hat rack. Reach down, grab his fetlock, and tell him to heist. When he does, move your foot, then let him put his foot back down." Rate did just that, and on the command "Heist," Mage obediently lifted his foot.

"See how easy that was. If you're going to work with horses, you've got to get a little horse sense yourself. Remember that, boy."

"Yes, Pa."

Easy enough for Pa to say, but Mage hadn't been standing on his foot either. 'Course Pa's idea had worked. If Mage wasn't so dumb, it would never have happened. The other horses never seemed to step on him, or if they did, they moved just as soon as he gave them a shove and told them to get over. Boy, his foot didn't feel any too good either. Mage sure was heavy enough, and it felt as if the dumb animal had leaned toward him, thereby putting extra weight on that foot. Well, he'd know what to do next time, if he was unlucky enough to have a next time.

Nineteen hundred! The change of a century. While large cities like New York, San Francisco, St. Louis, and Chicago celebrated this change with more than the usual festivities for New Year's Eve, in the small villages like Elsie, the passing of one century for another went virtually unnoticed. The farm folk could see no cause for exuberance. A man who had to be in the barn early to care for livestock had little time to be spending the night celebrating anything. Not that they didn't like a little diversion now and then, but there were more appropriate times to their way of thinking. Let the city folk squander their time and money. The farm folk couldn't afford to be that frivolous. What if one went to bed and the year was 1899, and upon awakening, it was 1900? One day or one year was pretty much the same—some better, some worse, with a man doing honest labor to provide for his family just as the good Lord intended.

The snow was gone, but the ground was still partly frozen, although the days warmed enough to give hint that warmer weather would soon be on hand. Ralph had spent a portion of the afternoon with his grandfather getting wood from the north eighty. Since the stoves still devoured a considerable amount each day, Grandfather said his woodshed was getting too low for comfort, and he'd get the wood before the roads turned into a mire of mud. That night at the supper table, Ralph related the events to his father.

"Pa, do you know how to tell when you get a full load on that springboard like Grandfather's?"

"I reckon when it's piled a certain height."

"Nope. That's not the way Grandfather does it. We kept throwing on wood, and then he'd pick up the back wheel. We'd throw on some more, and he'd do the same thing. Well, when he couldn't lift the wheel, he said he guessed that had better be a load, and we pulled out."

At that, Millie burst out laughing. "Leave it to Pa to have some gimmick like that. Guess he knew how much that driving team of his could pull without too much effort. See, Rate, you learned something."

Rate nodded his head, only he wasn't too sure just what he had learned. He'd heard Pa and Guy Sherman talking one day, and they'd said that Rate Setterington was a heap stronger than most men, so unless he got to be as strong as his grandfather, it wouldn't do any good to judge a load that way.

Pa had once said that Grandfather was stronger than either he or Uncle John. Why, he told of the time when his pa was young, there'd been a dance at Elsie, and two strangers had come by. These two had decided to break up the dance, but before they got started, Grandfather had hit the one who'd been full of all the big talk. The man dropped like a felled ox, and for a while, they thought he was dead. Grandfather had said that if the man ever came to, he'd never hit another man as long as he lived. Then, Pa had chuckled and said he guessed that didn't hold for him and John since Pa had always whipped them when he thought they needed it.

Ralph had wanted to ask his father just what it was that he and Uncle John had done that Grandfather had felt they needed to be whipped. He guessed maybe he shouldn't interrupt, but he'd try to remember to ask Pa some evening after supper when sometimes Pa felt like talking about the days when he was just a kid. He was five or six years older than Uncle John, so he'd had plenty of work to do.

Rate also wondered what his grandfather had been doing at a dance since he knew that both Grandfather and Grandmother looked upon dancing as something evil and were quite outspoken in their views on the subject. In fact, dancing was cause for a rather serious breach between them and Uncle John. It seemed that when there was work to be done, Uncle John's feet always hurt and he felt miserable, but let him get wind of a dance somewhere, and he'd be there for the first squawk of the fiddle until the last. Aunt Grace was just as bad. She loved to dance, and when she played the piano, instead of it being the sedate, pious church music, she played other more rollicking tunes like the ones Ralph had been given to believe were played in saloons. Bet back in the old days, Aunt Grace could have made a mighty fine dance hall girl.

Of course, Grandmother and Grandfather never failed to voice their disapproval, but Uncle John, unlike Pa, paid no attention to his parents' objections. In fact, he seemed to maliciously enjoy having them know that he danced whenever and wherever he could. Perhaps John deliberately flaunted his sinful ways—for to Horatio and Lovina, they were indeed sinful—as a means of getting even for some of those boyhood whippings he had resented so much and for the times when his mother and father had tried to interfere with his way of living when he was already a married man, making his own way in the world.

Certainly John and Milford were not one bit alike. Millie never crossed either of his parents, not even to take his wife's part in some rather minor disagreement. Because Millie was desperate for parental approval, he could never bring himself to disagree with his parents' wishes, and while he perhaps secretly admired John's spunk, he let it be known that he did not agree with his brother's lack of respect for Horatio and Lovina. In fact, from the time of being boys, this had been a bone of contention between the two.

It was only a few evenings later when Millie, chores done, a satisfying meal under his belt, felt like expounding somewhat on his early life. Rate had started the ball rolling by asking, "Pa, how old was you when you came to Elsie?"

"Well, boy, I was two years old. Don't recollect much about the journey myself," he added with a chuckle. "Your grandfather and your great-grandfather John Setterington came here to Elsie in 1867. They opened a general store and run a livery stable right there on the south side of Main Street, west of where Van Deusen's grocery store is now. I don't know as I know what made them decide to leave Canada or why they came to Elsie, but they did.

"Grandfather had told Pa that whenever he wanted to go back, they'd settle up right then and there. Well, one day in 1871, Pa was cultivating corn in north of where they built the school. He owned a whole section there, and Grandfather owned a section to the east. Grandfather sent word to Pa that he wanted to take inventory right then because he was going back to Canada. Pa had to drop everything and do like his father wanted. Didn't make any difference that Pa had been smack-dab in the middle of a job. When Grandfather wanted something done, he wanted it done then. There used to be a high board fence between the livery stable and the store so's the horses could get a little exercise. It was my job to take those horses to the creek north of town each day for water. I wasn't very big then, but I had a pony to ride, and I guess the job could have been a whole lot worse."

Rate figured it didn't sound too good to him. He bet some of the horses gave a lot of trouble, so he ventured, "But, Pa, didn't they sometimes run off?"

"Not usually. We had one old mare that kind of lorded it over the rest, and she was dependable. She'd have gone there and back by herself, I think, and the others sort of followed her. If we got a new horse in, it might cause some trouble, but somehow me and that old pony managed. Guess the horses knew it was their only chance for a drink, and once they'd had their fill, they were content to come back to their hay and a ration of grain."

Millie paused a moment, then went on to explain, "Our first home in Elsie burned. Don't know just what caused it, but I presume sparks from the chimney. Sometimes, chimneys weren't put up as good as they ought, and this could have been one of those. I was about twelve when Pa decided to build kitty-corner to the west of your grandma Smith's. At that age, I was considered man enough to handle a yoke of oxen, so Pa sent the hired hand and me to fetch a load of shingles from Potter's mill. Jake told me when we left, 'Now, Millie, when we come back, watch your oxen, for they'll be dry.' Kid fashion, I hadn't known what he meant, only I didn't ask any questions either.

"On the way home, I went to sleep up on top of the shingles. I knew the team would follow the wagon ahead of us. Well, sir, I didn't wake up until that wagon was going down the embankment to the river. It tipped over and scattered those shingles all down the slope and ended in the river. I went into the river with shingles on top of me. Thought I'd like to drown, but Jake hauled me out. Then and there, I knew what the hired hand had meant. I should have unhitched the oxen back down the road apiece, led them to the river for a drink, and then hitched them up again. Those oxen had been mighty thirsty, and they'd just taken the shortest route to water.

"By golly, by the time we got the load set to rights again, it was nigh unto morning. In fact, I got home just in time to set down to breakfast. Believe you me, I was beat. Pa didn't say much except I was given to understand that my chores still needed doing. I knew right then and there that sleep or no sleep, Pa intended me to do my day's work just the same. When I kept busy, it wasn't so bad"— Millie chuckled—"but if I sat down, I'd almost fall asleep."

"Your father certainly wasn't very understanding," volunteered Miney.

"I don't know as I'd say that, Miney. I suppose he felt it was my own fault, and I guess it did teach me something. I lived through it, so no harm was done."

Millie was always quick to defend his father from any criticism, no matter how insignificant and small. However, Rate was inclined to agree with his mother. He could just visualize the stern look on his grandfather's face reminding Pa there was chores to be done. Grandfather certainly had his own ideas about how to bring up boys. Shirking work didn't enter into the plan not one little bit.

Ralph had heard his father and his grandfather talking about a barn raising on some property just outside of the village that belonged to his grandfather. He'd heard the older men talk of such things, but there hadn't been any around this neck of the woods since he'd been old enough to be interested. He was in hopes Pa would let him tag along and watch this one. He figured he'd wait until that very day to ask permission; otherwise, Pa'd have too long a time to think about it, and then, he'd likely think it was no place for a small boy.

Pa had stopped in on their way home from town one afternoon, and Rate had seen the piles of lumber, and he had watched a man using a broadax. The axe had looked funny to him at first with its crooked handle, but when he saw the man deftly square off a beam from what had once been a round tree trunk, he could see the wisdom behind it. My, but there was a lot of lumber. The shingles had been piled to one side along with the wide boards, which he supposed would be siding, only there was a lot of other pieces, which he had no idea what they were designed for. He had hoped fervently that Pa would let him come to watch so's he could find out where they went.

He'd heard Ma and Grandmother and Aunt Grace talking about feeding all those men, so he knew Ma would be busy all day too. Like as not they'd expect he and Blanche to go over to Grandma Smith's. Not that he didn't like to go there, 'cause he did. Grandma always had cookies for him, and she smiled a lot. If he did get into some little mischief, she never seemed to mind awful much. He guessed she must be getting awful old, and she had been poorly of late, but she still was always good-natured and glad to see him. Besides, she usually took his part when he and Blanche disagreed. He guessed she liked him just as much as Blanche or even a mite better. She was sure some different than Grandmother. But even if he did like going there, just this once he'd rather stay and watch the workmen. Maybe he should ask God to give him a little help. Ma always said that if we prayed in Jesus's name, God would answer our prayers. Well, he guessed he'd put it to the test.

The day dawned sunny and bright. Millie was in exceptionally good spirits, so as everyone was bustling about getting victuals packed in the buggy, Rate brought up the question foremost in his mind.

"Pa, can I stay with you and Ma and watch the barn raising?"

"I don't know, boy. Think you could stay back out of the way? The men will be too busy to have a boy underfoot, and you could get hurt."

"Millie, hadn't he better go to Ma's along with Blanche? I'll have no time to keep my eye on him and neither will you."

"The lad might learn something. Tell you what, Rate, you can stay, but the first time I have to speak to you, off you go to your grandma's."

"All right, Pa. I promise I'll look out, honest, I will. See, Blanche," he hissed, "you said Pa wouldn't let me 'cause I was too young. Lot you knew."

"Who'd want to stand around all day watching some old barn being built anyway? Bet I have more fun. I might even get to bake cookies, and just see if I bring you any."

"And I suppose I'll care."

"You two hush up and get in the buggy," ordered Miney. "Your pa's coming with the wagon and team. Hurry now, I don't have all day."

What Rate didn't know was that Blanche had already seen more than one barn raising, so it wasn't the novelty to her that it was to him.

What in future years would be the Schenck place was bustling with activity. Horatio had bought the place from his brother-in-law, Lem Bingham, and since it had no barn, he had decided it would increase the value of the property enough to go through the bother of building one before selling the place. Men and rigs were arriving in droves. More women joined Miney, Lovina, and Grace in the tent erected for them. Men working hard had ravenous appetites, and the women were starting early. They knew there'd be a steady stream of men for coffee and a plate of food or a piece of cake or pie, and since not all would be working at the same time, they'd eat in shifts.

Rate watched the swarm of men with interest, each man intent upon some job, each seeming to know what he was to do. One man, the master carpenter, was everywhere at once, issuing orders and supervising construction. Rate watched the assembling of the bent on the ground. The beams had been notched so the others slipped into place and were pegged with a cylindrical wooden peg, which had to be driven into the bored-out hole. As Ralph watched the bent, which was to be the east end of the barn, taking shape on the ground, he began to wonder just how they'd ever get it upright and in place. Guess maybe he now understood what "barn raising" meant, for if they built all that stuff laid out on the ground, somehow, it was going to have to be raised into place. Boy, supposing one side was longer than the other? Somebody sure had to know what they was doin'.

In a shorter time than he had thought possible, the bent was finished. Now he'd find out how they'd get it up. From somewhere, there came a lot of ropes. The ropes were tied to the topmost beam of the bent, the center one strung through a pulley on what he later learned was called a gin pole. It was a tall pole set in the ground in what was to be the inside of the barn. Some of the men carried pikes, which to the lad looked like something out of medieval history, since they were long, stout poles with a spike at the end. With no instructions given, each man seeming to understand his job, the men assembled along the bent, one row on a side.

Ralph watched in awe as the men who were to handle the ropes started taking up the slack, and then began pulling in earnest to "Heave! Heave! Heave!" in steady rhythm. Slowly and surely, the top of the bent began to rise. As it neared its upright position, the men with pikes began to push and brace, giving it the support needed to stay in position. When it was upright, ropes to the east and ropes to the west were snubbed around metal braces driven diagonally into the ground.

In the same manner, the next bent was put into position, and Ralph watched as the men skillfully pegged timbers linking the two bents securely in place. He sensed, rather than saw, the ripple of relief that spread through the workers when this task was done. The addition of the second bent lent stability to the structure.

All right, now he knew how they raised this much, but they still had the rafters to be put in place. The thought occurred to Ralph that someone sure had to be pretty bright to know how to do all these things. The lad realized once again that adults knew a lot about many things. My, but he did have a lot to learn. Pa sure was smart. Rate had watched him, and he seemed to know just what to do and when.

Ralph watched the other bents raised into place, propped, and supported; next, he watched as the ridgepole and rafters were raised and nailed into place. He thought the men who crawled around on these rafters were very brave, and he wasn't at all sure he'd have liked their job. After the roofboards were in place, the job of shingling didn't seem all that bad.

By late afternoon, much of the barn was completed. Of course, it was a rather small one, not nearly the size of the barns built on farms. There was still part of a side on which to finish putting the siding, and the doors still had to be made and hung, and the roof wasn't quite finished, but it was nothing that a small crew of men working together would have any trouble finishing.

Toward the end, Ralph had begun to get restless, and he'd liked to have asked Ma when they was going home, but he daren't. He also knew better than to hunt up his father to ask him. He had seen a few men and rigs leave, but he supposed since it was Grandfather's barn, it was more than likely that Pa and Ma would be one of the last to leave. He was still glad he'd come. Bet Blanche hadn't learned half as much as he had today.

School was almost over for the year, and Ralph was looking forward to vacation. Still, he guessed he'd sort of miss having so many friends to play with. He liked playing anti-I-over. At noon hour, they'd choose up sides, and then one group would go on one side of the woodshed, one group on the other. Someone would roll a ball over the peak of the roof to the other side yelling "anti-I-over." If a person over there caught the ball, they ran to your side, trying to touch as many of your players with the ball as they could while the two teams changed sides. If you got caught, you had to change teams. Sometimes, one team would get down to only one or two players. Rate was getting pretty good at catching the ball when it rolled off the roof, only he couldn't always catch someone from the other team because he wasn't all that fast at running.

'Course, he'd liked it in the winter when they'd played fox and geese in the snow. The older boys played prisoner's goal, but they wouldn't tolerate the smaller children playing with them—said they only got in the way. Well, next year he'd be bigger, and he just knew he'd be able to run faster, so maybe the big boys wouldn't laugh at him for being small and slow.

CHAPTER 3

Rate sat on the porch idly toying with a stick, his thoughts engrossed with the litter of pups he'd seen yesterday. Don Sherman—better known as Curly—his best friend, had told him Wally Hiers's bulldog had whelped a few days ago, and sure enough, when he went over there, Mr. Hiers had let him look at the silky, wiggling mass of puppy flesh, so entwined it was hard to tell which head went with which body, legs, and tail. One pup, a little larger than the rest, had been snoozing fitfully, his belly obviously full, and his littermates crawling over his topside bothered him not in the least. Rate had wanted to pick that one up in his hands; he could almost feel the silky smoothness of the close- fitting puppy hair, and his fingers itched with longing.

Mr. Hiers had said they were too little to be handled, and old Maudie wouldn't take kindly to someone picking them up while they were so little; however, the longing in his heart didn't seem to go away.

Rate wanted a pup.

More than anything, he wanted that contented little fellow who didn't get disturbed even if his brothers and sisters did crawl all over him. He'd asked Mr. Hiers how much they cost, and he had told Ralph he would sell him a pup for a dollar and a half.

"Might's well be five," Rate said aloud. "Pa wouldn't let me have a pup—he says dogs are more bother than they're worth, and since Grip disappeared some time ago, he likely wouldn't want another dog. And I don't have more'n a few cents anyhow."

He sprang up and dashed into the house unmindful of how he slammed the door and dashed upstairs to his bedroom. He dug down into a drawer for the box in which he kept important things.

He dumped the contents on the bed. There were a couple of shiny stones, a porcupine quill, a jackknife with one blade broken, some string, some nails, a rivet or two, a pencil stub, a ring from a horse's harness, and two pennies. Ralph stared at the pennies. It would take 148 more to have the price of a pup, even if Pa would let him have one.

Once more, he sat down disconsolately. Golly, a boy needed a dog, something he could call his own, something to love that would love him in return. There just had to be a way.

That night at supper, Rate announced to his father, "Maudie, Wally Hiers's bulldog, had her pups, Pa. I went over an' see 'em today. They sure are the nicest pups I ever see."

"Well, now, are they? What made them so special?" asked Millie, his eyes twinkling.

"They…they…well, they was nice and fat for one thing, and ole Maudie, she's takin' awful good care of them, an' this one ole fella is bigger'n all the rest."

"They aren't very old, are they?"

"No, Pa, they're tiny yet. Just got their eyes open a day or so ago. Ole Maudie didn't want nobody touchin' them yet, so's Mr. Hiers said I couldn't hold one. When they get bigger, he's gonna let me," he stated proudly.

"Ralph, you aren't to make a nuisance of yourself," put in Mina.

"I won't, Ma. Mr. Hiers, he told me I could come over anytime I liked. Honest, he did. Pa, could I have a pup?"

There, the words were out. To be sure, this wasn't quite as he'd planned it, but still, he'd got the question out. Now, he waited breathlessly for his father to answer.

Millie watched the face of his young son and saw the unspoken pleading in those brown eyes, which were so like his own. He forced himself to refrain from allowing a smile to creep to the fore as he seemed to ponder a moment, then asked, "Will Wally just give you the pup?"

"Not… not exactly. He wants a dollar and a half for one."

"Boy, do you have a dollar fifty?"

"No, Pa, but I thought—"

"You don't have a dollar and a half? Just where did you expect to get the money to buy this pup? Money doesn't grow on every bush as you well know."

"I have part of it," Rate volunteered.

"Well, Rate, just how much do you lack?"

"A dollar and forty-eight cents."

At that, Millie could contain himself no longer; he burst out laughing. Rate did not share his father's humor, and his downcast eyes gave hint that he would have shed tears if he could have managed to be alone.

"Millie, don't tease the boy. This is important to him," chided Miney. "Ralph, did you have a plan for the rest of the money? A dollar and a half is a lot to ask for."

"I know, Ma."

"Not a dollar and a half, Miney, a dollar and forty-eight cents." Millie chuckled again. "Tell you what, boy, since your ma seems to cotton to the notion of you having a dog, perhaps she'd be willing to pay you to pick strawberries. There's quite a patch on that south forty. What do you say, Miney?"

"I hadn't given it much thought. I hadn't intended to go traipsing clear over there for strawberries when I'll likely have all I can take care of right here. Do you think we could sell them?"

"I'll ask next time I go to town. Seems like one of the stores could use them, if not both."

"If we can sell them, I guess I could probably pay Ralph a cent a quart for the picking."

"Hear that, boy? I think you can consider you have a job."

Ralph's face beamed. It was like the sun breaking through a dark storm cloud and shedding its quick, bright light upon a hopeful world. The supper he had been pushing around on his plate began to disappear as his appetite miraculously returned.

He hated picking strawberries, but when the drudgery of the job was balanced against a pup of his very own, the scales most certainly tipped in favor of the pup. At this moment, Rate truly believed there was no job he would not have tackled with a vim since he would be allowed to purchase a pup with the money.

Picking strawberries was not the greatest job in the world; in fact, it was rather backbreaking work—the hot sun beating down mercilessly, making one feel a little like a roasting pig except there was no one to turn the spit, so the picker gets overdone on one side. Be that as it may, Rate was sure a cent a quart was a fair price. That meant he had to pick 150 quarts of berries. Well, 148 if he took into consideration that he already had two pennies. Then, the awful thought came to him like a blow to the head. What if there weren't that many strawberries? A hundred and fifty quarts was an awful lot of berries, that was for certain, so supposing he still didn't have enough money?

Maybe Ma would help him out if he did some extra chores for her. He couldn't rightly think of what, but there must be something he could do for her, and maybe she'd give him a nickel. But no, Ma was awful close with money. Besides, it was only a little short of a miracle that she had not only consented to let him have a pup, but had almost volunteered to help him get it. No, he could expect no more help from that quarter. Ma always said if you had a problem of any sort, you should take it up with the good Lord in prayer. Well, it seemed he now had a problem, so he guessed he'd better ask God to make sure there were 150 quarts of strawberries in that old patch. God had sure enough seen that he got to the barn raising, maybe He'd think a pup was important too.

That night, Ralph's sleep was beset by dreams. He held a brown wiggly puppy in his arms while the pup's little pink tongue proceeded to wash his face, and its needle-sharp teeth nipped at his ear. He awoke and, for an instant, wondered what had happened to his pup. Then, he remembered. He didn't have a pup; he could buy one if he could earn the money—the gigantic sum of $1.50—to pay Mr. Hiers.

"Please, God, please help me," he murmured as he drifted back to sleep.

*****

"Ma, when's Pa coming back from town?"

"I don't rightly know, but I expect he'll be here by suppertime. That man just never misses a meal," she added.

"Do you suppose he'll remember to ask about selling the berries?"

"If he told you he would, he will. Now, stop fretting. Your moping around won't change a thing. Why don't you just go outdoors and play and get out from underfoot?"

"Can I have a cookie first?"

"Here, take one and leave."

My land, but that boy had been a nuisance ever since he'd wanted that pup. He hadn't really teased Millie to find out if they could sell the strawberries, he knew better than that, but the question had been there, unspoken on his face each day, patiently, although solemnly, waiting for his father to make a trip to town. Well, Millie had left right after dinner, and for once, Ralph had expressed no desire to go with his father. She supposed that while he was anxious to know, he had a fear that neither of the stores would want to buy strawberries. Poor lad, that pup was certainly the most important thing on his mind right now. She knew Millie would never give Ralph the money if the stores wouldn't buy the berries. She wouldn't want to give him the money outright, and he already did most of the little chores for her that he was capable of doing, so she had no ready solution. In fact, she too was apprehensive, wondering if the boy was going to get what he already considered "his" pup.

A light rain had begun to fall, so Ralph came back into the house to play. He commented to his mother that Pa should be home most anytime, but knowing that she had begun supper, he wisely stayed out of her way.

When Blanche came downstairs to take the cheesecloth off the table, put the plates in place, put the flatware around, and do the things young girls were supposed to do to help their ma, she hissed, "What makes you think you need some old dog anyhow? Bet no one wants to buy strawberries. Why, most everyone has their own."

"Not the ones who live in town, and not even all the farm folk. I heard Mr. Fizzell say they weren't going to have any this year, so why wouldn't folks buy them?"

"Maybe they don't have the money. Not everyone can buy just any old thing they want, you know. Bet you don't get a pup."

"Bet I do. Just wait and see. I'll show you, and when I do get him, you better watch out, or if you kick my shins, he'll bite you."

"Ha! Lot you know. Any dog of yours would be too dumb to do anything."

Drat it all. Blanche was probably right. He'd never be able to earn the money. He sat down by the south door where he could keep watch of the road and could see his father approaching long before the rig reached the driveway.

"Ma, Pa's home. Shall I go help him take care of the team?"

"You stay right here in the house. It's raining quite hard now, and one person getting wet is enough. Like as not he'll have to have a change of clothes when he gets in the house. Besides, it won't take your pa long, and then you can find out about the berries," she added kindly.

Rate looked at her in wonder. How in thunderation had she known what was on his mind? He certainly had been awful careful not to say one word about strawberries or pups even if that was about all he'd been thinking of just lately. Sometimes, mothers were a wonder, and sometimes they were awful nice to have around.

He guessed his ma was kind of special even if she did favor Blanche. Lot he cared. Pa liked it 'cause he was a boy, and who'd want to be a silly old girl anyhow?

Millie came in shaking himself like some huge dog.

"Gettin' mighty wet out there, Miney, but we do need the rain. Things was gettin' awful dry. Wouldn't hurt a bit if it kept this up all night."

"Here, I brought you a dry shirt. Almost looks as if you need dry trousers too."

"No, this will be fine." He slipped into the dry shirt, quite unmindful that his underwear was damp too. "Something smells good. Don't know why, but a good rain always whets my appetite."

"A good rain or anything else. Milford Setterington, you always have an appetite for two men."

"Now, Miney, would you want to feed some persnickety soul who didn't do justice to your fine cooking?"

"Oh, sit down and stop soft-soaping me. I know how much you think of your stomach."

The meal was nearly over when Rate brought up the subject foremost on his mind.

"Pa, did you find out?"

"Did I find out what, boy?"

"'Bout the strawberries," he explained patiently.

"What about strawberries? Looks like there'll be a good crop this year," he added, the crinkles around his eyes showing.

"Millie, don't tease," chided Miney.

"Pa, didn't you ask like you said you would? Can't we sell strawberries anyplace?"

"Oh, that. Well, I spoke to both stores, and either one will take all we can bring in. They'll pay us eight cents a quart too. So, boy, now all you have to do is get them picked."

"Golly, Pa, that's just great. They'll be ripe soon, won't they?"

"In a couple of weeks or so, they'll start turning, unless we get too much cold weather."

Rate felt as if the weight of the world had been lifted from his shoulders. He just knew he'd get that pup now. He guessed he'd better start thinking of a name for him since it had to be extra special, for this was an extra special pup. The pup would be his, all his, and he'd be the one to teach it lots of tricks, and he'd take his dog with him everywhere he went. His dog. My, but those words had a nice ring. Something that was to be his very own and not shared with anyone.

A few days later, Ralph listened with interest as Millie and Cash Waldron discussed a colt.

"Millie, I've broken and trained a lot of colts for you, but this one has me stumped."

They were leaning on the gate watching a sleek-looking bay cavort around the barnyard. Muscles rippled under the glossy coat. He watched a leaf glide to the ground, ears forward, a wary look in his eye, then he danced away on dainty feet.

"In what way? He appears all right to me."

"Most of the time he is. Most of the time he handles as nice as an old mare, but then he explodes, and I mean just that. Once he's over it, he settles back down and drives like a dream. No, sir, Millie, you'd best get rid of him as soon as you can."

"Badger Jay! Come here." Millie whistled. Obediently the colt trotted over to the fence, nuzzling his nose in Millie's outstretched hand. "Seems gentle enough, Cash. Sure it isn't just that he's a mite more frisky at times?"

"It's more than that. I've handled too many horses not to recognize a bad actor when I see one. You'll have nothing but trouble with him, mark my words. Seems a shame as he is a beauty."

"Think I'll try driving him for a spell and see for myself."

"Don't say I didn't warn you."

Millie did just as he told Cash; he hitched up the colt, and on the first outing, all went well. Badger Jay drove as steady as anyone could wish, just as though he'd been driving for years. However, this proved to be the lull before the storm.

Mina and Millie were going to town, and Ralph asked to be dropped off at Sherman's. When Millie brought the buggy around, Miney asked, "Isn't that the colt Cash told you not to drive?"

"Ye-es," admitted Millie, "but I drove him day before yesterday, and he behaved like a charm. Cash always did tend to be somewhat pessimistic."

"Millie, he kind of scares me. I wish you'd taken one of the others."

"It'll be all right. You'll see."

Miney hesitatingly got into the buggy. Ralph handed up a large basket of eggs to his mother and then hopped onto the back.

"All set, Pa." And with that, they left the yard at a brisk pace.

"See how well he moves, Miney. This one paces naturally. We never had to put the training hobbles on him once. He's a mighty fine animal. Someone will give me a good price for him."

"The sooner, the better," muttered Miney, a worried furrow between her eyes.

They turned the corner east onto the Ridge, and as they neared Sherman's driveway, Millie pulled the horse in to stop. The buggy had not quite stopped when Rate jumped off. Then, he heard his mother scream. Badger Jay was releasing all his pent-up fury in the only way he knew— head down, heels flying—with Miney holding her basket of fragile eggs up in the air, saying, "Do something, Millie, do something."

"I'm trying, I'm trying. Whoa! Whoa, there." His hands were steady on the lines, his words soothing yet forceful. "Steady, Badger Jay. Steady, boy. There now." The animal quieted, and off they went; Millie was looking as though nothing unusual had happened, but Miney's face was drained of all color, and she was busily mopping her brow with a white handkerchief, which quite matched her face.

When Rate explained it to Curly, he said, "Ma sure did look funny holding that basket of eggs just inches above Badger Jay's flying feet yelling at Pa to do something, and all the while Pa just sat there calmly talking to the horse like nothin' was wrong at all. Bet Pa never drives Badger Jay again when Ma is going with him."

"Wasn't you scared?"

"'Course not. I knew Pa could handle him," he boasted.

"Wisht I'd a got here in time to see it," came the disappointed sigh. "Suppose he'll act up when they come back by?"

"Naw. From what Cash says, he's likely to drive all right for days, but then he'll explode again. Sure seems a shame, him bein' such a looker an' all."

Millie was never one to admit he was wrong or that he had possibly made a mistake in judgment, so he was not about to admit that he had misjudged the colt, and Cash's observations had been more astute. He sold Badger Jay as soon as possible at a ridiculous price if one was to judge only by the appearance of the colt in the stall or pasture. However, he had told the man what to expect, since Millie was one of the more honest horse traders. It was not his fault if the buyer had felt Millie was exaggerating because Millie obviously didn't know much about horses. Millie was to learn that in a few months' time, Badger Jay had had two more owners. A born outlaw? No one knew. Millie secretly felt he was lucky to be shed of him although he would have denied having such thoughts had anyone bothered to ask.

Blanche had gone with her grandmother to spend the week with Aunt Ruby. Mina had been giving it thought for some time now that she would like to go visit her sister Ettie in Traverse City. Now seemed as good a time as any because if there ever was a lull in her work, it was now. Ethel Putman could come in by the day to get Millie's meals while she was gone. There wasn't likely to be a hired man until haying season.

After talking the matter over with Millie, it was decided Miney and Ralph would leave on Tuesday. When Lorin heard of it, she mentioned it to Georgie, who promptly wanted to come along. Mina wasn't all that enthused because her nephew sometimes seemed to be even more peculiar than her half sister. So far, he hadn't held a steady job but worked here and there—he was between jobs now. He would quit a good job when he got a little money ahead and then not work until he was broke again. Miney often wondered where he got this trait since Norm always worked although he did spend a lot of what he made on drink. Well, maybe it would be handy to have a young man along to help with the valises, and he could perhaps help look after Ralph. That boy was just not one for sitting quietly for very long, and he had the biggest bump of curiosity she had ever seen. He wanted to know how everything he saw worked. 'Course Millie was rather strict with the lad, so Ralph seldom got in anyone's way, and he didn't pester with a lot of questions; however, not much escaped his eye.

She just knew he would become bored long before they reached Ettie's, so maybe if they had a few minutes' stop someplace along the line, Georgie could take him into the depot just to give him a chance to stretch his legs and a change of scenery to boot.

Although Miney was right and Ralph had become bored, he was less trouble than she had imagined. Of course, it had helped immensely when the conductor had taken a liking to Ralph and had taken him on a tour of the train, even going into some of the other cars. Ralph had excitedly told his mother every incident on the excursion. Then too he had been shown where the watercooler stood at the back of the car, and it was simply amazing how often he worked up a dreadful thirst—almost as if he was in the middle of the Sahara. Naturally, being the outgoing child that he was, he smiled at the other passengers as he sauntered down the aisle and even said hello to some; so on about his third trip, some of them struck up a conversation. He came back all excited because one rather elderly lady had given him a cookie while another had produced a piece of stick candy—his favorite, wintergreen—which he elatedly showed his mother.

"Goodness, Ralph, I thought I had taught you better manners. Don't you know that you are not to accept gifts from strangers?"

His face fell for a moment, then he said brightly, "But, Ma, they aren't exactly strangers. That made the third time I see 'em."

"*Saw*, not *see*."

"Saw them."

Miney laughed at his logic.

"Aunt Miney, there's something in what he says. Besides, this really isn't like meeting some stranger out in the open. Those old ladies think he's cute, and you'll have to admit he doesn't hang back like some youngsters. He's always got a ready answer."

"You're right there, Georgie. I guess there's no harm done. Ralph, did you mind your manners and thank them properly?"

"Oh, yes, Ma. I 'membered, just like you taught me. They even told me their names. The candy lady was Mrs. O'Hare, and the cookie lady was Mrs. Evans. They aren't going as far as we are," he confided.

It had taken the entire day, but they finally arrived in Traverse City. Ettie had not come to meet them, but her husband, George Curtis, along with their sons, Glen and Free, was there when the train pulled into the station. Glen was nearer Blanche's age, so Ralph rather looked up to him just because he was older, and yet, even though Georgie was much older than either boy, Ralph did not look up to him as someone he would want to be like. Free, although nearer to Ralph in age, was too quiet and had little to say, so Ralph made no attempt to get acquainted with this cousin.

The next couple of days passed quickly. Ralph liked Aunt Ettie just fine. She was kinda small like Grandma and rather plain looking, but she treated him right well. Uncle Doc—George had once been a practicing physician although he was now an attorney—was exceptionally nice. During the evenings, he took the boys places and certainly did much to make Ralph's stay enjoyable. Ma, he guessed, was having a good time just visiting with Aunt Ettie, who was her own sister, not a half sister like Aunt Lorin and Aunt Mary.

Ralph had known that Aunt Ettie had a telephone because he had been nearby when Uncle Doc had called. The thought of being able to talk to someone who was so far away intrigued the lad. He mentioned this to Glen. Thus it was that the next day when Aunt Ettie sent the boys downtown on an errand, Glen stopped into the drugstore and asked the clerk if he might use the telephone. He gave Central the number of his home and, when his mother answered, explained the reason for the call.

Then, he gave the phone to Ralph.

"Aunt—Aunt Ettie?"

"Yes, Ralph. Where are you?"

"We're at a drugstore," he almost shouted.

"Ralph, it isn't necessary to holler. I can hear you perfectly well."

In a more modulated tone, "I can hear you too, Aunt Ettie. My, this sure is something. Just think how far away I am."

"Yes, Ralph, I know. The telephone is a marvelous invention, isn't it?"

"Oh, my, yes. Glen says I gotta go now. We'll be back shortly. Bye, Aunt Ettie."

Gee whiz, he'd talked on a telephone. Why, Aunt Ettie had sounded almost like she was standing right beside him. He'd known her voice right off. Goodness, just wait until he got home and told Curly that he had used a telephone. There were quite a number of them in use in the village, but thus far, not many lines had been strung into the country. Sure was amazing how a person's voice could go over the wire. Someone had to be powerful smart to have figured it all out.

*****

"Mina, where's that boy? Just lately he's never around when I want him. Where's he go all the time? He does his chores then skedaddles off so fast I can't catch him to do anything else."

"Why, Millie, every day he's been going over to that south forty to check on those strawberries. I thought you knew."

"You mean he traipses clean over there every day just to see those strawberries? No, I never dreamt that was what he was doing. What in tarnation for?" Millie looked completely perplexed.

"He's making sure they're getting ripe. Now, don't laugh, he is absolutely serious. He's afraid they'll get ripe early and he will miss a few quarts. Millie, that pup is all he thinks of. I've never seen a child so obsessed with anything."

"Well, I'll be darned. When he gets his heart set on something, he really goes whole hog, don't he? Think he'll stick to pickin' so he'll earn enough money?"

"If there's enough strawberries, Ralph will pick them. He may get sick of the job, but the thoughts of that pup will keep him going. I'm certain of that. My only concern is what will happen if there isn't 150 quarts. Do you realize what a disappointed young lad we'll have?"

"Let's not cross our bridges afore we get to them."

Miney knew there was no need to pursue this line of questioning because she would get no further opinion from Millie.

She pushed back a stray tendril of hair with the back of her hand. The palms were flour-covered where she had spread a thin coating on the board in preparation to roll out cookie dough. She paused a moment, watching her husband return to the barn. His shoulders were broad, his stride long; he was a powerful man who actually enjoyed physical labor, but a man extremely set in his ways. She knew he had set forth the criteria by which Ralph was to get a pup, and in no way would he alter any of the conditions. His stubborn English heritage would not let him pamper his son in any way nor give help where he deemed it unnecessary. No, poor Ralph would have to earn his dog with no outside help except God.

Ralph and Miney had spent a lot of anxious hours all for naught. The strawberries flourished. There was ample rain, and when the berries were large, a warm June sun softly kissed them to a deep-red, sweet-tasting and juicy. Ralph picked with a will. He zealously counted and recounted his growing pile of money. The nearer he came to the goal, the more he worried whether there would be that many quarts.

As all things must come to an end, so must the season for strawberries, and with its close came the pup to the Setterington household. Ralph christened him Bruno, and while no one exactly appreciated the first few nights when the pup howled his loneliness, he settled in quite well.

If anyone noticed that Rate often slipped a piece of meat from his plate to the pup wiggling under his chair, they said nothing. Actually, the pup was exceptionally well-behaved in the house as though he knew with a certainty that any infraction of the rules would result in him being cast outside quicker than a body could say *scat*.

Blanche had been wanting a bicycle for several weeks since some of her school chums were getting bicycles now that they had the same size wheel front and back and were much easier to handle than the old-fashioned kind had been. She had mentioned it to Pa and Ma, rather hinting that she could even ride into town as they weren't always too keen on her driving because some of the driving horses Millie kept were a little on the skittish side. Honestly, they never thought she could do anything unless it was connected with work. Ralph had been driving since he'd started school, and he wasn't even tall enough to throw a harness on a horse yet, so Pa always did that. Anyway, they were always afraid she'd get hurt just because Pa had known a family whose little girl got dragged by a runaway horse—seems she'd tied the lines around her waist so's she wouldn't drop one—and she'd been killed. Well, Pa said he didn't want anything like that to happen to his daughter. Actually, Blanche felt that her mother was behind the whole thing. Ma always seemed to worry about her, but she sure put up with a lot from Ralph without worrying.

Anyway, she'd broached the subject of a bicycle hoping for one for her birthday. Ma had been anything but enthusiastic, but Blanche felt that was just because Ma was so all-fired close with money. She'd tried to be extra nice to her father, knowing that he would be the one worth winning over.

Whether all of Blanche's thoughtfulness paid off, or whether Millie had intended to get her a bicycle all along, she never knew. However, her birthday did bring her a nice, new, shiny bicycle. For once, what Ma and Pa gave her far outshone any other present. She had the book *Jessica's First Prayer* from her grandmother, and Grandfather had given her a five-dollar gold piece, but it was the bicycle she appreciated most. My, it was beautiful. She could hardly wait until she could learn to ride it well enough to ride into town to show it off to her friends. She was certain it was the nicest one she'd ever seen.

Blanche had not reckoned with the condition of the roads when she had envisioned riding a bicycle into Elsie swiftly and easily. The Ridge Road was a rather sandy affair, and where the wheels of the buggies and wagons went, there was usually a rut, not always the straightest since often the horses sort of picked their own way, and the next team just naturally followed the same tracks. Blanche was to learn that between the wheel tracks, it was too soft, and the hard, narrow bike tires sank in far enough to make it virtually impossible to pedal. Trying to follow the ruts was almost as bad.

Besides, if she rode into town, Ma was sure to think of something she needed from the general store, so Blanche had to contend with a basket hanging on the handlebars, swinging back and forth, making steering more difficult and sometimes whacking her on the knee.

Then, there was the gristmill hill. Just as she crossed the long wooden bridge, with its board sides, which slanted across Maple River, Blanche always began to pedal furiously, hoping to gain enough momentum to enable her to make the hill. It was always the same. Even though she stood on the pedals and put all her weight on them, just shy of the top, she came to a standstill. Somehow, it always rankled to have to get off and walk the rest of the way. She hated to be bested at anything.

Of course, coming down the hill on the way home atoned for the ignoble ascent. She'd take her feet off the pedals even if it didn't look ladylike and let the bike fly. It was glorious! Down the hill, around the curve, and then quickly start to pedal to get over the bridge and up the incline to make the turn by the cemetery. Somehow, this always made the ride home exciting, which in turn made the whole trip worthwhile.

*****

It was election year once again, and Ralph had often heard his father and other neighbors talk politics when they met in town. Sometimes, he hung around to listen, but much of the talk was too deep for him, so he usually wandered off a ways to look in store windows or hang by his legs from a hitching post or to look over the teams and driving horses tethered along the street. My, some of those horses sure were pretty, and those fancy harnesses! He sure liked all those shiny buckles, the white rings, and the bridle rosettes.

Politics was a big issue once again. McKinley received the Republican nomination without any difficulty, and this time his running mate was to be Theodore Roosevelt, governor of New York. Teddy was a nationally known figure since "Colonel Teddy" had received a notoriety of sorts at San Juan Hill during the Spanish-American War.

Since the depression had ended in 1897, the Republicans were a strong force indeed. The best the Democrats could put up as an adversary was the already once defeated William Jennings Bryan with Adlai Stevenson for vice president. The Democrats had opposition to imperialism and the gold standard as a platform, whereas the Republicans upheld the gold standard. The Republicans also had prosperity on their side. McKinley's "full dinner pail" speeches did much to keep the support of the nation.

Millie and the neighboring farmers were no exception. They basked in the rising prices for grains and all farm commodities. They were not about to gamble with some new ideas in the White House when the present ones seemed to be doing much to improve their station in life.

Mina sat by the south dining room window doing some mending. Seemed as though there was always something wrong with Ralph's clothes—a missing button, a three-cornered tear, a torn suspender, just anything to keep her busy with a needle.

Of course, Millie was right near as bad it seemed. That man not only lost buttons, but they often got torn off where he caught them on something, so they always took a little of the cloth along with them. Miney disliked patching more than she did the original sewing, and she had no love for that.

She wished she could have been working on the rug she was crocheting, since she really did love to crochet. Time always slipped by rapidly when she was doing something she thoroughly enjoyed, and it did drag at times like this. She laid the shirt down in her lap a moment and looked out the window. Then, she chuckled. My goodness, that boy certainly enjoyed his pup.

Ralph took off running, and the pup chased after him as fast as the short legs would propel the fat, little body, yapping as he went. Then, Ralph dropped to the ground, and the pup tried to lick any part of his master's exposed body he could reach, and judging from the sounds, his needlelike teeth sometimes found a bit of flesh to grab since Rate hollered, "Bruno, you stop that. Don't be so rough. And don't you grab my pants. Ma will be awful mad if you tear them. Now, stop it. You hear?"

Miney laughed again. She guessed Rate never intentionally tore his clothes, but things just always seemed to happen to that boy. He attracted trouble like honey did flies. She had thought his most troublesome years would have been the baby years when there had been all that extra washing, or the toddler time when he had gotten into everything; but now, she wasn't all that certain. Still, he was a lot of help to her.

Blanche could help if she wanted to. She always dusted and helped with the dishes, and she could now iron some of the flat things—that is, unless they were starched; but she was gone a lot, and when it came to churning butter, well, she hated to do that as much as Ralph did, and they were forever squabbling over whose turn it was. In the summer, she helped feed the baby chicks or ducks or geese, if they raised any. Still, if a body was to be perfectly honest with oneself, Ralph was often more of a help than a hindrance and perhaps a mite more helpful than Blanche, Mina thought grudgingly.

Mina smiled as she thought of her daughter. Blanche was growing prettier all the time. She was tall, slender, with such a smooth, creamy complexion; her dark hair was fine and thick, and her brown eyes were so dark that at a distance, one couldn't see the pupils. Millie's had never been that dark, but Father Setterington was the one with the black eyes. Perhaps in some ways Blanche reminded her a little of her father-in-law; she certainly had a big dose of his stubbornness and pride. Well, if life would only be as successful for Blanche as it had been thus far for Horatio Setterington, she would be a mighty lucky girl.

One day, Blanche asked her mother what Grandfather did for a living. Blanche had been giving this a lot of thought for quite some time. She recollected that he had once owned a livery stable and general store, a furniture store and funeral parlor, but now he owned no business, and yet he seemed to have plenty of money. Not that he or Grandmother squandered any, but they could buy whatever they took a notion to.

Mina explained to Blanche that Horatio loaned money, and people paid him interest on the loans; he also bought farm property or city lots that were being sold for taxes throughout Clinton County and some in Gratiot and Shiawassee County, which he sold for a tremendous profit; he also raised running horses.

This bit of information impressed Blanche—the fact that owning money could earn you enough to live in quite as comfortable a manner as her grandparents did. She knew Horatio often came out to the farm to help Pa with some of the work, but it was because he liked to work and not because he had to. He often remarked that a man got soft if he just sat around. Grandfather certainly wasn't soft. He was twenty-three years older than Millie, but he still could match his son in the field.

Blanche knew that Grandmother had a hired girl come in by the day to do the cleaning and laundry. She felt that Lovina did the cooking simply because she enjoyed cooking, and she prided herself on her baked goods. Remembering, Blanche felt that Grandma Smith made much better cookies, and Ma's pies were better, but Grandmother did make awful good bread.

Grandmother not only had her own hired help anytime she wanted help, but Blanche had heard Ma and Pa talking about that ever since Aunt Ruby and Uncle Mac were married, Grandmother had paid for a hired girl for Aunt Ruby. Uncle Mac made nine dollars a week as a bookkeeper at Masons, and that didn't quite allow the luxury of hired help. However, Lovina was not about to let her only daughter do all her own housework, and if Mac couldn't afford it, Lovina could. Horatio had not objected to the situation although it probably would have made no difference if he had. Where her daughter was concerned, Lovina was even more unmovable than was usual. There had been some talk of Aunt Ruby and Uncle Mac moving to Big Rapids because Uncle Mac had the offer of a job in a bank. Maybe then they could afford their own hired help.

Blanche decided a person could do a lot worse than pattern himself after Rate Setterington. Pa resembled him in looks although he wasn't as clever in business, partly she guessed, because he was softer and let his heart rule some of his dealings. She guessed that even though she was a girl, she would like to be as astute about business as her grandfather.

*****

Once again, Jim Keenan was back to help with the haying. Like as not, his brother, Merval, would be here at least part of the time too. Millie liked hiring the brothers since they were both good workers and never slacked off on any job they were set out to do. Jim was an exceptional man with a team, but while Merval lacked his brother's ability with horses, he more than made up for it in his quickness in the field.

Ralph was chatting with Jim while the latter spliced one of the small ropes used in the barn during haying.

"Jim, don't you never go home?"

"Nope."

"You still got a ma and pa, haven't you?"

"Well, Ma's still alive, and I got a step-pa. I ain't seen 'em for quite a spell. If Ma comes to visit Frankie, I allus go to see her if I can. Missed her last time though."

"Whyn't you ever go home?"

"Rate, it's like this. Me an' my step-pa, we don't see eye to eye. I weren't much of a kid when I left home for good."

"Don't your step-pa like you?"

"Don't reckon I know. Don't recollect my own pa, but I allus figgered he wouldn't have whupped me like my step-pa did. S'pose I asked for some of it, but I allus figgered he delighted in whuppin' me. Anyways, I got a good laugh the day I left home for good."

"What happened?" asked Rate.

"I'd been out huntin', an' I wuz comin' back to the house. By the back door stood this swill barrel where we dumped garbage an' such to use when we slopped the hogs. Well, a neighbor's cow stood there with her head down in that barrel. I pulled up my gun and filled her backsides with buckshot. She let out a beller, an' in her hurry to get her head outta that barrel, she somehow got it caught on her horns. Wal now, she couldn't no more see where she was gain' than a bat in bright sunlight, so she just took off blindly. I thought she looked funnier'n hell until I saw she was headed straight for our privy. She hit it smack-dab in the middle, an' over it went. She had busted the barrel off, so now she took off for home. It was then I heard the screechin'. Seems like old man O'Hare, my step-pa, had been sittin' in that outhouse, and he was lettin' loose with a string of cusswords to fair curl your hair. Wal, Rate, I figgered I had better make tracks, so I just turned and left. Ain't never been back."

"But, Jim, how'd he get out?"

"Danged if I know. But I wasn't about to wait and find out. I was only about fifteen, and he'd have near killed me. He was just lucky it didn't fall on the door. He'd have had trouble crawlin' out a hole," Jim stated laughing. "No, I don't reckon Ma's had too easy a life with him an' his temper. She's allus had to work hard, and they've allus been dirt poor. I'm just glad Frankie got out of there. It's a lot harder on a girl not to have nuthin' than it is for boys. 'Sides, I like not stayin' in one place too long. Workin' for your pa is fine, but after a while, I'm ready to move on. Don't know if I'll ever want to settle down."

Rate decided he was glad he didn't have a step-pa 'cause he sure didn't want to leave home. Maybe Ma and Pa did favor Blanche, but they were good to him in lots of ways. Why, he always had spending money each week even if sometimes Ma only gave him a penny. Whenever Pa went to town, he got to ride along, and sometimes, Pa would buy him a stick of candy without him even askin'. He liked things just as they were.

The haying season was almost finished. The last two days had been unbearably hot as only a cloudless July day can be. The men had soaked their shirts in short order as the sweat poured out of their skin much as water goes through a sieve. The horses were frothy wet where the harness laid, and small rivulets of water ran down their sides. They moved with methodical slowness needing to be urged to go from one haycock to another, content to wait while the men pitched the hay onto the wagon. Millie had cut this field two days ago, and it had cured fast enough to be raked yesterday. He had used a dump rake to put three swathes from the mower into a straight line, and the two hired men had pitched them into cocks to make it easier to pick up today.

Mina was even more uncomfortable in her kitchen than the men were in the field since the only breeze there was came from the south, and none of it relieved the additional heat from the cookstove in the kitchen. Well, the men had had a good midday meal; there had been six extra hungry mouths, but since the men had their own chores to do, they'd go home for supper. Therefore, she made up her mind that their meal was to be warmed-up leftovers. There was enough of the beef roast left, she'd slice that cold; she'd warm up the boiled potatoes and gravy, they'd have leaf lettuce from the garden with sugar and vinegar, and she'd open a jar of peaches—she still had a few jars left—and there was pie enough for Millie and Father Setterington and Ralph. She and Blanche could do without, or if Blanche wanted, she'd have to split a piece with Ralph. They'd have milk for the children and cold tea for the three grown-ups.

With a sigh, she sat down in the rocker by the south dining room door to take a moment's respite. Wouldn't you know it, what little breeze there had been had died down, so she absently picked up a cardboard fan, a means of advertising from Van Deusen's grocery store, and gently fanned her face. She wondered where the children were. Blanche was no doubt upstairs doing some embroidering; she had started a pair of pillowcases, and that girl just never was content until she finished something. Ralph would be somewhere around the barn or riding on one of the hay wagons. Millie might even be letting him drive a team on the wagon. She'd heard Ralph ask his pa about it after dinner, but she hadn't heard what Millie's answer had been, if indeed he had bothered to give one.

That was one of Millie's traits that never failed to irritate her, his being so closemouthed and never taking the time to answer her questions or discuss things with her. Like as not any discussion they were to have about folks in general was pretty much one-sided and often ended by Millie saying, "Miney, keep still." Those words always raised her ire partly because she knew that any further attempt to draw her husband into conversation would meet with stony silence and partly because she hated being spoken to in that tone of voice. Her own father had been much more voluble and had often recounted some humorous incident at the supper table. Not so with Millie. To him, a meal meant a time to replenish his stomach's needs, and hardly a place for a great deal of conversation. On occasion, by the time he was down to his dessert, he might talk some, but Miney always suspicioned that was just to prolong being at the table for the extra piece of pie. That man was a bottomless pit when it came to devouring food.

When the menfolk trooped into the house for supper, Miney was putting the last of the victuals on the table. As Horatio walked by the kitchen cabinet, he noticed a pan half full of milk that had clabbered solid in the heat.

"Mina, are you going to throw this out?"

"Yes, Father, I was. It was only milk from yesterday, but even with the cellar, it is hard to keep in this weather. It was sour this morning, and just look at it now, clabbered solid."

"But, Mina, it is still good to eat. Do you mind if I have some?"

"Of course I don't mind. I just never thought of anyone wanting to eat it," said a flabbergasted Miney.

She watched in awe as her father-in-law spooned a sizable helping onto his plate and, immediately after grace, set in with a will to devour the soured milk. Millie seemed not to notice, but the children watched wide-eyed with disbelief as their grandfather ate with gusto. From the looks on both of their faces, one could safely assume the dish did not appeal to them. Since Millie paid no heed, Miney presumed he had seen his father eat clabbered milk before. Oh, well, she guessed it wasn't going to hurt him any, only she knew for certain that what he didn't eat would get fed to the hogs.

Horatio had left for home, but before he had taken his leave, Ralph heard him say, "Milt, I'm glad that was the last of your hay. It's too hot, and there's something in the air. Doesn't even smell right."

Rate sniffed the air, but all he could smell was the smoke from the chimney and the carcass of a chicken that had died a couple of days ago, around which those big green blowflies were swarming; he knew the next day it would be crawling full of fat white maggots.

"You're right, Pa, something don't feel quite natural. It's mighty still tonight, and even the robins have shut up and aren't calling for rain anymore. Don't know quite what to make of it."

"Nor I, Milt, but I don't like the feeling."

Ralph asked Millie about it after his grandfather left, but Millie only said, "It's something I can't put a finger on, boy, but mark my words, something is going to happen."

That night, before Millie went to bed, he went out on the south porch to look at the still somewhat lightened sky. A man who arose at four thirty each morning went to bed these summer months before total nighttime darkness shrouded the land. He stood for a few moments gazing intently to the southwest, looking for clouds above Sherman's woods. At this time of year, any sudden, severe storm was more than a little likely to come from that quarter; however, he could see nothing unusual in the softly illuminated sky where the rays of an already setting sun still unveiled a light cloud cover.

"Miney, something's brewing. I feel it in my bones."

"What do you mean?"

"I think we're in for bad weather, a hailstorm, a cyclone, hard thunderstorm, or something."

"I don't see anything unusual," said Miney as she came out to stand beside him, slipping her arm around his waist. "Still, the hogs were scratching their backs today, so it could likely rain."

Ignoring her remark, Millie muttered, "I don't like waiting for the unknown, so I wish it would hurry up."

The black, ominous clouds hung low as they swirled and fought for position, first one on top, then another seemed to take its place as if stirred violently by an unseen giant hand. Mina had been nervously watching out the south door, noting the roll of thunder like the beat of distant tom-toms, sometimes an incessant rumble summoning nature's mighty forces for an attack on puny Earth. She remembered Millie's prediction of last night, and she wished he would get home before the storm broke, knowing full well that he was powerless to change the will of God, but it would make her feel easier to have his stalwart frame seated in his chair, nonchalantly watching the foreboding signs.

Nothing ever flustered Millie. He firmly believed what would be, would be, so there was no use to fret. She didn't know if she wished she could be more like him or not. She knew she often worried, and yet, it made not one whit of difference in the outcome. Millie was wont to scoff at her fears, so she usually tried to hide her feelings, but sooner or later, she could keep still no longer. Now, she had to control her emotions as best she could, for there was no cause to alarm the children. Ralph sat on the floor contentedly playing with Bruno. The pup knew something was amiss because his mind seemed to wander, and Ralph had to repeatedly urge the pup to retrieve the ball he was throwing.

Ralph certainly did take an interest in that pup. Bruno had been fetching a ball for several days, and Ralph was now trying to teach him to roll over. It made no difference to him that Millie had told him the pup was too young. Ralph knew this was the smartest dog God ever created, so he wanted the pup's education to start early. At least the pup was keeping Ralph occupied, so he apparently paid no attention to the heralding of a storm. Not that he'd have been afraid—he was too much Setterington to ever admit fear.

Goodness, it did seem that both he and Blanche took after Millie's side of the family much more than they did hers. Pa and Ma had been so much easier going and not nearly as stiff-necked and proud. 'Course, they'd never had as much either, but they had been mighty good parents, and she loved them both.

Here came Blanche. If she had noticed the black clouds, she certainly didn't act worried. Blanche might be petrified, but her dignity would carry her through, and no one would be able to detect any fear in her speech or actions—once again the Setterington pride.

The wind was starting to blow in strong gusts.

"Ma, should Ralph and I put the little chicks back in their coop? It looks dreadfully stormy."

"Oh, land's sakes, yes. I'd forgotten that we had let them out for the day. Ralph, you leave Bruno here while you help Blanche. Oh dear, do hurry."

The children left to find the settin hen with her brood of twelve chicks. They had raised a corner of the A-frame coop to let the mother hen wander. Much to their relief, the hen had sensed the offing of a storm and had returned to the safety of the coop with her chicks settled comfortably under her wings. They carefully put the corner down and hastened to the house, and only just in time because the first large drops of rain began to pelt the ground furiously.

"Ma, did you get the windows closed?"

"Yes, Ralph, I did that while you were outside. I wonder where your father is?"

"Comin' like a streak o' lightnin'. Just look at him travel," marveled the lad.

Ralph was right. Millie had let the team have their head, and the wagon, loaded with bags of grain, bounced wildly on the rough road. It seemed the team wanted to be home as much as Millie did. He pulled the wagon onto the barn floor; closing the big barn doors proved to be troublesome as the wind was now increasing in velocity, and it took some effort to fasten them in place. Miney noticed that Millie lost no time in getting the horses unharnessed and turned out, stopping to close the granary door on his way to the house. The rain still held off, the large drops not having been enough to lay the dust.

"Millie, I'm glad you're home," greeted a relieved Miney.

"So am I. I didn't relish getting soaked to the skin. I think that this wind is going to blow up a good rain, and I'm not sure what else. It's too danged hot and too humid."

"Guess you were right last night. Goodness, Millie, the windows are rattling, and just look at the trees."

Miney had looked out to see the box elder south of the house trying to touch its topmost branches to the ground. The poor old cottonwood creaked and groaned as did the stalwart elm behind the woodshed. Even the sturdy house seemed to tremble, perhaps in fear of the furious hand who guided these massive forces.

"Millie, are we going to be all right?"

"Don't fret none. It will soon blow by. A wind this strong can't last," was the optimistic reply.

"Pa, the door came loose off the corncrib," volunteered Ralph. "Boy, look at it rain!"

The rain had finally come. Sheets of water, driven by the wind, swept across the countryside. The barn, hardly more than a hundred yards away, could scarcely be seen. The crackling of lightning increased, the thunder tried to outdo itself with each rumble louder and longer than the one before. Blanche and Ralph watched in fascination, hardly noticing that Bruno kept close to Rate or to Millie, going from one to the other; Miney couldn't help showing her anxiety, and when one loud report seemed exceptionally close, she jumped and cried, "Millie, did anything here get hit?"

"I don't think so," he replied, looking out the north window to see what he could of the buildings. Just then, a loud, sustained, agonized screech reached their ears.

"Pa, there went a limb off the cottonwood!"

"I see it, boy. We were clean lucky. It missed the house completely."

"Oh, Millie, is it ever going to quit?"

"Reckon so. Most storms do, don't they?"

"I mean before it blows down some of the buildings."

"Well, you didn't say that. I think the worst is over. At least the wind is dying even if the rain hasn't let up any."

"Pa, look at the corn," came from Blanche. "It's all tipped."

The field south of the house was planted to corn, which had been its knee-high by the Fourth of July, but now, it looked sick indeed. The fury of the wind had tilted the young plants, so they leaned at an angle of close to forty-five degrees. The leaves hung limply like a hound dog's ears.

"It'll straighten up some, Blanche, but it sure don't look good now. Just knew that hot, humid air would bring some foul weather sooner or later. Just be glad nothing worse come of it. I've seen the time when we had hailstorms that stripped all the leaves off the corn. Think we can consider ourselves lucky this time."

The storm finally abated, the wind no longer blew with ferocity, and the rain fell softly and gently; the sun finally peeked through the clouds, and across the sky was as beautiful and perfect a rainbow as one could wish to see.

"Ma, come look," called Blanche. "See, isn't it pretty?"

"Yes, Blanche, it is. Must be that the storm is over for certain. God paints a right pretty rainbow, doesn't He? Millie, what are you fixing to do?"

"Thought I'd take a gander and see what damage was done besides this cottonwood. Rate spoke of the door off the corncrib. I hope we didn't lose any shingles off any of the roofs."

"Ralph, where do you think you're going?"

"With Pa. I want to see too."

"There's no need to have both of you getting wet shoes, so you stay right where you are."

Ralph looked his displeasure, but said nothing. He stood on the porch and watched as his father headed for the barn.

A survey showed that except for some small branches off the elms and box elders, the door off the corncrib, and the large limb off the old cottonwood, they had no major damage. Millie felt they were lucky.

When he learned that in some places barns and sheds had been blown down and trees uprooted, he was indeed thankful their losses had been so minimal. Mina was just plain relieved and hoped there was not going to be another storm like this one for a good long time.

CHAPTER 4

Miney was in a hurry. She lifted the iron lid of the cookstove and peered in with an exasperated sigh. "I just knew that wood was too damp to burn like it ought," she mumbled to herself. She removed the lid and poked the small sticks of kindling with the poker. As if to pacify her at least temporarily, the fire began to burn a little brighter. "Suppose I might just as well add another stick so it can be drying out."

Doing this, she then set the kettle filled with potatoes into the place where the lid should have gone. It would mean a blackened pot to clean, but there was no time to brood over that now. At the rate the fire was going, dinner was going to be late since the meat had hardly started to sizzle, let alone fry good; and if there was anything she didn't like, it was half-fried meat. No, sir, she wanted hers well-done with drippings to make nice brown gravy.

Mina checked the potatoes. At least they were beginning to boil. Must be that last stick of wood hadn't been as wet as the others.

"Blanche, it's time for you to get the table set."

"All right, Ma. Do you want me to cut the bread too?"

"Well, I don't know." Miney knew that the slices Blanche cut were often lopsided, starting with a nice narrow slice but ending with a width of nearly an inch. Still, how was the girl to learn? "Go ahead, but try to cut straight down through the loaf like I've shown you."

"I do try, only it just never seems to come out right," she lamented.

"Oh, I'll need milk for the gravy."

"Do you want me to go get it?"

"I think I'd better. That pan was really full, and I'm afraid you'll spill it. Goodness, here comes your father already. Well, he'll just have to wait for once. G`uess it won't really hurt him any, although I suppose he's most dying of hunger now."

Miney turned the meat in the pan—it was frying well enough now, checked the potatoes and found they had a ways to go yet; then, she left for the cellar.

In a matter of moments, a shrill scream pierced the air. Millie dashed into the house, Rate tight at his heels, and as the next scream came, they dove for the cellarway door.

"Miney, what on earth is the matter?"

"Oh, Millie," she half sobbed, pointing toward the south wall. "A snake, a big snake, coiled up in the pan where the milk should have been. It just looked at me a minute, and then it slithered away. It was this big." She held her arms as far apart as they'd reach. "And it was this big around." She used her thumb and forefinger to measure the diameter of a silver dollar.

"What color was it?"

"A malted color, sort of mottled. What was it, Millie?"

"Just a harmless old milk snake. Your screaming probably scared him worse than he scared you. There, it's all right," he said clumsily, patting her shoulder. "You know a milk snake never hurt nobody. Don't quite know how he got in though."

"How'd he get in the safe? And into my pan of milk?"

A safe was simply a screened-in, portable cupboard with shelves for storing perishable food. The door was standing ajar, and there set the gray enameled pan, empty of its contents, mute testimony as to the presence of an intruder.

"It was a whole pan full too," wailed Miney.

"Now, Miney, no great harm's done." He sniffed, then asked, "Do I smell something burning?"

"Oh dear, my meat. Or is it the potatoes?"

Miney rushed up the stairs to salvage the midday meal.

Rate had watched the entire episode silently although he found it a trifle humorous. Ma wasn't usually one to get that scared over an old snake, but it sure must have taken her by surprise. He wondered if the snake had found a hole in the stone wall and had left by the same way or if it would show up another day in the cellar. Much to Miney's relief, the snake disappeared, and it was as though the episode had only been a bad dream.

Blanche had remained at the top of the cellarway steps. She hated snakes with a passion. My, but she felt she was to be eternally thankful that she had not been the one to go fetch the pan of milk. Just supposing she had been the one to open the safe and find that ugly head, with the flicking tongue and beady eyes staring at her. She shuddered, her arms covered with goose bumps, and she felt cold all over. She fervently prayed that the snake was gone for good. She didn't care if Pa did say they were harmless, she hated them, and they gave her a creepy feeling. She wasn't about to admit that the feeling was akin to fear, she simply knew she never wanted to have such an encounter. In fact, she and Miney were both so upset that they ate very little. However, both Millie and Rate remained undaunted, and the food disappeared as usual before their voracious appetites.

A harmless old milk snake was of no concern to Millie or Ralph. These snakes were a frequent visitor around the barn. Millie supposed they ate mice and rats although some people swore the snakes milked the cows, so if they had a cow that was off on her milk, they laid the blame on the poor snakes. Sometimes, when pulling straw for bedding from the huge stack behind the barn, with the hooked tree branch worn smooth and shiny from use, it was not uncommon to pull a snake out with the straw.

In some parts of the county, there were still a number of rattlesnakes, but Millie hadn't seen one on his own farm in years. Why, he'd mind hearing Dave Watson tell about when Dave first settled on his farm, they had a lot of marsh grass to put up for hay. The rattlers were so bad they had to wrap the horses' legs with burlap bags to protect them from the snakes. Hadn't been completely safe for the men either, but they had worn high tops and kept a mighty close watch on what they were doing. Millie had to admit that he had a healthy respect for a rattlesnake and wasn't exactly sorry there had never been but a straggler or two left on his farm. 'Course, he supposed womenfolk were different, and he couldn't blame Miney for being upset. Like as not it was the unexpectedness of it since Miney wasn't usually that easily excited.

Blanche had gone with Millie to the neighbors. Now, for some reason, she was driving home in the light springboard wagon by herself, for Millie was nowhere to be seen. When she pulled into the yard, the pup, Bruno, ran yapping toward the wagon. Just before Blanche halted the team, the pup got too close to the back wheel. When it struck him, he limped off yelping his indignation and pain.

Ralph came bounding off the porch, and the pup, sensing this was going to be a sympathetic person, limped ki-yiing to his master.

"Blanche, you've cracked his hide! Just look. You've cracked his hide."

Ralph took hold of the pup's loose skin, pulled it away from the body to show his sister, looking at her accusingly.

Blanche climbed down from the seat of the wagon.

"Oh, Ralph, he's all right. Bruno's hide has always been loose like that. Honest."

"Tweren't neither. You've cracked it. Here, Bruno, poor fellow. Why'd you run over him?"

"I didn't mean to run over him. He just ran right under the wagon."

"You could have stopped," he accused.

"I'm sorry. Here, Bruno."

The pup had quieted with all this attention and now ambled over to Blanche to lick her outstretched hand.

"See, Ralph. He's all right. I didn't do it intentionally. You're going to have to teach him to stay out of the way."

"Are you sure he's all right?" the boy asked as an errant tear slid down his cheek.

"Of course. See, he doesn't even limp now, and his hide isn't cracked one bit."

"Well, if you're sure."

Ralph picked the pup up in his arms and headed back for the porch with Bruno trying his best to lick his master's face.

Goodness, thought Blanche, Ralph sure was concerned about his pup. Who'd have thought the pup would be that dumb anyway. At first, she had been afraid he was hurt badly. Now that she knew he was all right, it was rather comical. Cracked hide indeed. Bruno's skin had always been so loose, you could always get a good handful. Poor Ralph, he really did love that pup, and she was thankful nothing was really wrong. She wouldn't have wanted it on her conscience to have seriously hurt Bruno. Besides, she kind of liked the pup too. Even Pa seemed to like Bruno, so the whole family would have felt badly if he had been killed.

She guessed young boys just needed a dog to grow up with. Ma had even taken an interest in the pup and had shown Ralph how to teach him some tricks. Ralph had really been very patient and had taught him to sit up and speak. Ma said that when Bruno got a little older, Ralph could teach him to roll over, sneeze, say his prayers, and read the newspaper. Ralph just never doubted his mother one bit since he knew Bruno was of exceptional intelligence.

The dog was easy to teach, and between Ralph and his mother, they not only had a well-behaved dog, they had one who enjoyed showing off in front of an audience. He also enjoyed the tidbits Ralph sometimes gave him for a job well done.

Because Grandma Smith was feeling poorly, Millie had a telephone installed so Lorin could call Miney if she was needed. It took several days for the phone company to get the poles set and the phone installed; of course, even though they now had a telephone, the children were not allowed to use it. In Miney's mind, it was for adults only, and then only used when absolutely necessary. She never considered calling someone just for the sake of talking; besides, she didn't have time to waste.

When school started, Ralph had a new teacher, Barbara Hess by name. He didn't much mind. Miss Silvernail had been all right although she never laughed much. Blanche said she looked like a bird perched on a fence, and he often thought of that when he looked at her. Still, she'd always been nice to him. Now, Miss Hess smiled a lot more and often came out on the playground to supervise the youngest children. They loved her.

She even tried to make the rather drab schoolhouse look pretty by putting up pictures appropriate to the season. The windows had been built high, and when students were seated at their desks, they could not look outside. Of course, this had been intentional since the students were there to learn, not to gaze at the countryside. Anyway, she had some pretty pictures she put up all around the classroom. Sure brightened it up. She also said she'd asked the school board to replace the recitation bench since it was rough, and if a child was to slide along it, he might pick up a sliver. She wanted one with a seat that folded up like their desks.

Ralph was glad to be back in school. He liked learning new things. He worked hardest at learning to read because he wanted to get big enough to read books like Blanche did.

November came, and with it, election day. The people of the growing new nation turned out in remarkable numbers to make their choice. Once again, as a nation, they turned to the Republican party and reelected William McKinley as their president, and with him, Theodore Roosevelt became the vice president. For the second time, Bryan had gone down in ignoble defeat. Prosperity had made a very worthy opponent, and McKinley was the one who had prosperity on his side. The deck had been stacked in his favor from the onset.

Millie and his neighbors were exceedingly pleased with the election outcome. They foresaw continued prosperity for farm families. Prices for farm commodities had been holding steady, and they attributed this to the Republicans; they forgot that grain failures in Europe and other parts of the world had improved foreign trade, thereby creating a demand for these same commodities. People often believe only what they want to believe, and Millie was no exception. He was confident the good times would continue, and at least in this respect, Millie was much like anyone else—he enjoyed work, but he also enjoyed a just reward for his labor.

Christmas that year was even more special to Ralph. Since he was learning to read, Aunt Mary sent him some books as did Aunt Ruby. To be sure, he could read only a few words here and there, but he was assured that by the time school was out in the spring, he would be able to read them with ease. At least they had some pictures, so he could enjoy looking at them. Besides the books, Grandmother and Grandfather gave him a blackboard that stood on a frame. He'd never seen one like it; there was even a box of chalk.

Grandfather immediately asked Rate to do his sums and nodded his head in approval when the lad did the simple addition quickly and correctly.

Anyway, Rate figured he had been mighty lucky this Christmas. Of course, he hadn't got the ice skates that he had wanted so badly, but he did have some money that he was saving like a veritable miser. 'Course, Ma never gave him much at a time. Fact was, she'd only give him a penny to spend on Saturdays, and some of the time he just felt he had to spend it.

Wieners—how he did like wieners, and a penny was enough to buy one. Now, if Pa was to give him money, he'd like as not give him a whole nickel, so that way he could buy a wiener and have four cents left to put toward his skate money. Trouble was, just lately Ma usually beat Pa to it, and if Pa went to give him money, she'd always say, "I've already given Ralph his spending money." Sure. One measly old penny, yet he didn't dare complain.

It was one Saturday in January when Rate's grandmother found him counting his small cache.

"What are you doing, Ralph?"

"Counting my money, Grandmother. So far I've got thirty-eight cents."

"What are you saving all that money for?"

"I want some ice skates."

"Ice skates? Where will you go skating?"

"At school. At noon hour, the fellows go to the river to skate. Most everyone else has skates," he explained.

"Even those who are your age?"

"Yep. Curly Sherman got a pair for Christmas."

"Is it safe to be on the river?"

"Where we go, it is. Farther north, just afore the bridge, is the rapids, and that don't ever freeze over, I guess. But where we go, it is safe enough."

Lovina nodded and continued on to the kitchen where Miney was busy baking.

Before she left for home, she called her grandson over to her. "Ralph, can you carry this basket of eggs out to the cutter for me?"

"Yes, Grandmother. Soon's I put on my coat."

Ralph followed his grandmother to where his grandfather already sat in the cutter. As he handed the basket up to her, he felt something round and cold being pressed into his hand. He opened his palm, and there lay a shiny silver dollar. Eyes wide with wonder, he glanced up to say, "Th-th- thank you, Grandmother. Oh, gee, thanks a lot."

"Be sure and put it towards those skates."

With that they moved off. Ralph was certain his grandmother had smiled at him fondly, and even those cold blue eyes had looked warm. Oh boy, a dollar and thirty-eight cents. Why, that was nearly enough to get the skates. Maybe he'd be lucky enough to have them before the winter season passed.

My goodness, who'd have thought that Grandmother Setterington would have given him money just because he wanted some skates. Must be she did like him after all, for every once in a while, she'd do something nice when it was most unexpected. If only she didn't look so stern all the time. Of course, she often had a smile for Grandfather, but children just seemed to bring out her sternness. Even Blanche said she didn't smile much, and everyone knew she thought Blanche was quite the nicest one around.

His thoughts turned to his grandma Smith. My, but she was different. She just seemed to like children. Look how she'd taken care of Georgie when he was little; everyone said it was because Aunt Lorin was scared to handle him when he was small. Of course, this was long before he was even born since Georgie was a lot older'n Blanche even. Anyway, he'd heard Ma laugh and say Lorin held Georgie at arm's length, afraid to hardly touch him. Seemed funny that Aunt Lorin hadn't cared all that much for her own boy, but yet, she was always saying that she wished she had a boy like Ralph. Mighty strange. She had always been good to him and even treated him as good or better than Blanche. Ma had always said that Lorin never liked Georgie until he was older. 'Course Uncle Norman had always drank a lot and had changed jobs often, so maybe that had something to do with it too. Anyway, all the grandchildren liked Grandma, but he bet he liked her best.

Rate knew his mother was extremely worried about Grandma Smith because he had come into the kitchen, rather quietly for a change, and had found her crying as she sat peeling potatoes. She had hastily dried her eyes on her apron when she noticed him, and when he'd asked her what was wrong, she'd said that she was all right and nothing was the matter.

But he knew differently.

Grandma had been poorly of late, and he and Blanche had talked about how it was so much harder for her to get around, her movements were much slower and more calculated. Blanche had told him it was because Grandma was getting awful old, and when folks got that old, their body began to wear out. At least that was what Grandma had told Blanche.

He wondered why it had to happen to such a kind person as Grandma. Just didn't seem fair to him. She had been seventy-six on January 30. He had asked Ma what year that meant she'd been born in, and Ma had said 1825. The year made it sound awful old indeed, and he knew that seventy-six was older than his other grandmother.

Then, last night, Aunt Lorin had called. Ma hadn't said much to Pa in his hearing, but he knew from her part of the telephone conversation that Grandma had had a bad spell and that Aunt Lorin was going to spend the night with her. Tonight, it was to be Ma's turn, so she was hurrying to have an early supper and had told Blanche that she could do the dishes by herself. It still got dark quite early since it was only the first of March, and Ma wanted to be there before dark. He didn't think Pa was driving her, and he knew Ma disliked having to drive a horse after dark.

No one mentioned the word *dying*, but he had a hunch his grandmother hadn't long for this world. It made him feel depressed, the very thought of not having Grandma's kind, homely face to watch as she told him some story, not having her warm cheery kitchen to visit and her cookies to munch; he liked to watch her knit, since Ma never did, and the clicking sound of the needles was a soothing, comforting sound.

Mary Smith had always made the heavy black woolen stockings they wore in the wintertime. In a world where Ralph's wants always came in second, his sister's always given priority, it was little wonder he enjoyed the unselfish, kindly, little Scotswoman who did not have it in her heart to show any favoritism.

Of course, Ralph knew that Grandma tired easily, and he supposed she was ready for her home in heaven since then she would be shed of this tired, aching body and would be reunited with her loved ones. This last thought gave him some consternation. Since Grandma had been married to a man named Elisher Fuller, Aunt Lorin's and Aunt Mary's father, he wondered if she'd be reunited with him or with Grandpa Smith, who was Ma's father. Things like that were awful hard to understand, especially when one was only seven years old. He expected he could ask his mother, but like as not, it would only make her feel badly, so he guessed he'd better not.

Ralph was right. Mary Barnes Fuller Smith was tired; her poor body was no longer functioning properly, but even though she sensed that death would soon be a caller, she kept her thoughts calm and serene, comforted by the passage in the Bible: In my Father's house are many mansions. She would now have the wondrous eternal life that God's Word promised. She had no apprehensions, no anxieties, and the only regret she had was the prospect of leaving her daughters and grandchildren. She loved them dearly. Yet, it was inevitable. Hers had been a good life, and she thanked God for all the favors He had bestowed. If there had been any moments of doubt, any days of darkness, He had guided her safely through the storm and had seen her in the midst of the fold once more. This worldly life had become an unwelcome burden. Mary began to long for release.

Thus it was that on Tuesday evening, March 12, 1901, Mary Smith left this world quietly as she slept. The look of peace and contentment that heralded the transition was noted by both Miney and Lorin, who sat at her bedside. Mary had happily gone home.

Blanche and Ralph were told the following morning. Even though both of them had known for several days that this would likely be the outcome of Grandma's illness, it made the reality no easier to bear. Ralph didn't say a word but sat on the floor pushing a toy in an abstract manner, while he used his shirtsleeve to wipe a tear that now and then managed to sneak out from the brimming eyes. Even though he knew boys weren't supposed to cry, he wished he could resort to tears.

Blanche went back upstairs to her room. Ralph knew why. He knew Blanche would be crying out her grief in the solitary confines of her room. That was Blanche for you. She never wanted anyone to know that she ever cried over anything. Rate knew because he sometimes sneaked upstairs and caught her with her head buried in her pillow to muffle the sounds. For some reason, he had never told on her, and much of the time, no one else guessed she had been crying.

Ralph correctly understood his sister's actions. Blanche had gone upstairs to bear her grief in solitude. Her beloved Grandma Smith was dead. No more would she be waiting with open arms to assuage Blanche's grief over some confrontation with her grandmother Setterington. No more could Blanche sit in her warm, cheery kitchen eating some of Grandma's delicious cookies. All this was gone, wiped out in one brief instant. One moment Grandma had been alive and the next she had been with God. Blanche felt more than a little resentful that God had chosen now to take her grandma home. Didn't He know how much she, Blanche, needed her? Didn't it make any difference to Him? Ma always said that God knew best, and we must never question His wisdom. Well, what was she to think? Right when she needed her grandmother, God took her away.

Of course, she thought begrudgingly, Grandma had been feeling poorly for the past three or four months. Why, all this school year, Blanche had tried to be much more of a help and, since Christmas, hadn't even been able to stay with her, but she'd still stopped in after school because Grandma was always so glad to see her. If God had been a mind to, He could have made Grandma feel better. Perhaps Blanche had not prayed hard enough for her grandma's good health, and perhaps the prayers had not been all that regular. This made her feel a twinge of guilt. Maybe God would have left Grandma here to provide Blanche with the comforting love she so longed for if only she had prayed more diligently. With these thoughts, she cried as if the tears would never stop.

Ralph only remembered going to Ray Sawyer's funeral, and since Ray wasn't relation, it was hardly the same. Now, he was unnaturally solemn, fully realizing the gravity of the situation. The rooms of the house were packed. Grandma had had a lot of friends. No one was paying any attention to him. Ma was crying softly as the minister began the service. Even Pa looked sorrowful, and he was sure he'd seen Grandmother Setterington hastily dab at her eyes with her lacy handkerchief. Aunt Ettie, Aunt Mary, and Aunt Lorin were crying in turns. Blanche sat staring straight ahead, and he just knew she was fighting to keep back the tears. He paid little attention to what was being said. No one needed to tell him that his grandma was a mighty fine person—he already knew that.

At last, there was a final prayer, and then the people began to file out. Since they were family, they were the last ones to leave. Now, to the cemetery, and then it would be all over.

The black hearse, drawn by black horses, moved slowly and steadily west on Pine Street as the church bell tolled mournfully. It was only a block to the village cemetery. The hearse turned into the solitary drive situated in the center of the cemetery. Rate knew Grandma's lot was on the north end, right by the drive, because he'd been there with Ma to put flowers on Grandpa Smith's and Great-Grandfather Barnes's graves. He could see the mound of dirt and the opening while they waited for the pallbearers to bring the casket and place it over the opening. While the wind was cold and raw, the sun did peek from behind the clouds as the minister stepped to the head of the casket for the final words and prayers.

Soon, it was over. Rate watched as the coffin was lowered into the cold, bleak earth, but turned away as the men began to shovel the dirt from the pile onto the casket. Somehow, that act made it all seem so final, the thud of the half-frozen clumps striking the wood. He hated that sound. He was more than glad to move away, back to their carriage, and begin the ride home.

It was several days after the funeral when Blanche asked her mother what was going to happen to Grandma's house. Somehow, it was important to her not to have strangers cluttering up her grandma's house with its simple, homey furnishings.

Mary Smith had owned a small farm, some lots in the Tillotson Division besides the house where she lived with two lots and a barn across the street. Her four daughters—Mary, Lorin, Ettie, and Almina—were to share equally in the estate. On the counseling of his father, Millie decided some town property might be a good investment. Miney passed this bit of information on to her daughter, who felt much relieved. Grandma's house was to be theirs, and even if Grandma couldn't be there, she could sit in the house and remember the good times.

Therefore, by the time it was all settled, the farm and the lots being sold, it was decided that for two hundred dollars, Millie could buy the house and lots across the street.

Blanche finally had the courage to speak her thoughts to her mother. "Ma, I'll just never understand why God took Grandma. I enjoyed her so much, and I feel kind of lost knowing she isn't there for me to talk to anymore."

"Blanche, Ma was ready to go. Don't fret, child, God knows best. Ma had been in much more pain than she ever let on, and now, she has no pain. She missed Pa an awful lot these past few years, and I'm sure she was glad to see him. I know you will miss her. I'll miss her too. I've never known anyone kinder or more mild-mannered. Why, she just never lost her temper even when we were children, and Ettie and I did get into mischief now and again. She'd chide us or scold a little, but I never remember a switching. Even with Pa's boys, she was loving and kind. I sometimes wish I was more like her, but I guess I'm more like Grandfather Barnes, too outspoken and opinionated to always get along. Leastways that was what Ma always said. He died before I was old enough to remember."

"But, Ma, why didn't God see that we needed Grandma?"

"That is a very selfish thought. You should be asking yourself what was best for your grandma. Do you think she would choose to live here in pain when her husband was waiting for her to join him in heaven? Not to mention her own mother and father and, I believe, sisters and a brother."

"I-I-I guess not. But didn't Grandma love Ralph and me? And Georgie? And Aunt Mary's family?"

"Of course she did, sweetheart. She loved all of you dearly, but, Blanche, seventy-six is a lot of years to have lived. Remember Ma had had a hard life. She was born in New York State, you know, came to Michigan in a covered wagon when Mary was just a little tyke. Her mother was dead, so her father came with her and her husband.

Now, a covered wagon isn't the best mode of transportation. Guess probably Ma walked a good share of the way—that's one reason her feet always gave her trouble. It was already the first of November when they got to Vernon, and then, her husband just dropped dead. Pa lived in Vernon, and his wife was dead. He had four boys to raise, the youngest being Lorin's age. Since both of them needed someone, they started keeping company after Ma's year of mourning. Then, after she married Pa, he decided to come here to live.

"Why, the house I was born in was just a log cabin a block south of the main four corners. I remember that much. Ma worked hard all her life, and I expect she was just plumb wore-out. Oh, she never complained, but that was just Ma. Besides, dear, we are not to question why God does what He does. I'm not even sure that when our time comes, we will ever understand why He did things as He did. Don't suppose it really matters. The only thing that matters is that we lead the kind of life He expects of us, and then salvation will be ours, and we will one day all be together in heaven."

Blanche mulled these words over. She guessed Ma was right, and she was glad she knew Grandma was safe and happy in heaven. However, the ache in her heart was still there, and she knew it would be for some time to come.

Goodness. Blanche certainly was getting to be spunky and opinionated. Imagine questioning why God had done something. Miney hated to admit it, but at times like this, that stubborn streak of Blanche's reminded her of Mother Setterington. Oh dear, why did Blanche have to take after her? Well, perhaps it was just her imagination. Still, the older Blanche got, the more she had a mind of her own.

March had been colder than usual. Winter seemed determined not to relinquish its hold on the land. The sun managed to shine feebly on some days, but its efforts seemed too puny, and the snow still covered the ground with the only bare spots being on an occasional hilltop.

April was heralded in by fierce cold blasts instead of the usual warmer breaths of spring. The prolonged cold made lambing season more difficult than usual. Try as hard as he might, the number of lambs disowned by their mothers kept growing. An ewe is an especially unnatural mother; let her lamb get separated from her while it is drying off, and nothing you can do will make her accept the lamb and let it feed. Quite the contrary. She will butt and kick the lamb unmercifully each time it tries to suck, so the poor creature slowly starves. Often when giving birth to twins, she will accept one, but not the other.

This year, Millie had brought more than one lamb, looking more dead than alive, to the house in a wooden crate to set it on the oven door for warmth. It was always a little amazing how life seemed to return to that tiny body, which looked to be all legs, when it had become sufficiently warm. It didn't take much to put a nipple on a bottle and give the lamb warmed cow's milk. Their soft, high-pitched bleats filled the kitchen each time they became hungry. When they gained strength, they were taken back to the barn. However, they had to be fed four times a day for the next month or so if they were to live.

Millie decided Ralph was old enough to take on the responsibility of raising lambs on the bottle. He'd done right well taking care of the white pig. It was good for the boy to learn some responsibility at an early age. He'd been helping Miney for some time now what with the churning, carrying firewood, and turning the wringer; however, he'd never had anything to do that had to be done in the morning before school, but the lambs would have to be fed then. Millie would have to tend to the midday feeding, but Rate could feed them after school and before he went to bed. The boy was seven, so it was time for more chores. It was true he'd helped with the horses for a spell now, so Millie was sure he could take on the bottle-feeding of a few lambs.

When the final tally was in, Ralph had seven lambs to raise for which Millie had told him he could have one of the lambs as his pay. This seemed like a good proposition to the boy. Besides, he liked the soft woolly creatures and felt sorry for them because their mothers would have let them die.

Rate always had a soft spot in his heart for any young animal, wild or tame. He always felt badly if something died and was at a loss to understand his father's seemingly unfeeling acceptance of the way of life—some things lived and some died no matter how a person worked to make them live. All his life Ralph was to dislike losing an animal even though he knew he had done all humanly possible to save it from death.

Blanche prevailed upon her parents to let her drive to school for a few days since Grandmother and Grandfather wanted to go visit Aunt Ruby. It had taken some doing, but Blanche had finally convinced both parents and grandparents that she could certainly be trusted with such a reliable mare as Topsy.

It rained most of the night, but with the coming of dawn, the rain ceased, although the clouds were black and scudded ominously across the sky. They hung so low that Blanche felt hemmed in as she started for school. Golly, maybe it hadn't been such a brilliant idea to drive to school this week; she could have stayed with Fern Wooley, only Blanche had failed to inform anyone that Mrs. Wooley had extended the invitation. She shivered. The wind was still cold. Sure didn't seem like April. When she crossed the river, she noted the rain of last night had swollen the artery considerably; it wasn't far from reaching the bottom of the bridge.

Mr. Cooley at the gristmill had been watching the river. It was still rising. A couple of inches more, and it would reach the planking of the bridge. Giving the matter some thought, he decided the village should be told in the event there was someone who had to go west to get home. That old bridge wasn't all that good anymore, and if the water kept rising, it wasn't going to be safe. In fact, the turbulent, swirling river just might take it out, or at least destroy the middle portion.

Blanche was busy writing a theme for English when someone came to the door and spoke to the teacher.

"Does anyone here have to go home west over the gristmill bridge?" asked the teacher.

Blanche raised her hand.

"But, Blanche, I thought you stayed in town with your grandparents."

"Not this week, ma'am. I drove."

"Goodness, child, then you had better hurry. The river is rising fast, and they are afraid the bridge might go out."

Blanche left immediately. She ran most of the way to Grandfather's, taking the shortcut through Grandma Smith's backyard. She was half crying as she got Topsy, who seemed to move at a snail's pace, out of the barn and hitched to the buggy. She didn't even take time to close the barn door, she just clambered into the buggy, picked up the lines, and started for home. Try as she would, she could not get Topsy to hurry. She even hit the horse lightly with the whip, but after a few yards at a slow trot, Topsy dropped back to her rapid walk. Time seemed endless. Blanche just knew she'd never make it to the river in time.

After what seemed an eternity to the frightened girl, she reached the gristmill hill; and from this vantage point, she could see the swirling, frothy water of the river hungrily clutching at the pilings supporting the wooden structure that now looked frail indeed. As they approached the bridge, Blanche could see that the water had already risen some four or five inches above the planks. She pulled Topsy up to survey the situation. What should she do? Was the bridge safe, or would it give way when she was part of the way across, letting her fall into that dark, raging river? After a moment's indecision, Blanche urged Topsy forward.

"C'mon, Topsy. The longer we wait, the worse it gets."

The horse hesitated, put a tentative foot forward into the cold water, then stopped.

Blanche slapped the lines. "Please, Topsy, oh, please, get me across."

The old horse edged forward, slowly feeling with each foot as she put it forward. Twice she fell to her knees, whinnied in terror, got back up, and steadily moved ahead. Blanche closed her eyes. That was worse. She was in the middle now and could see the torrential waters.

"Please, God, help us across."

Blanche was crying in earnest now. Topsy, as if sensing they were nearly across, speeded up, and as soon as her feet struck land, she surged forward to a fast trot with no urging from Blanche. When Blanche reached home, she laid her cheek against Topsy's neck and cried.

Millie and Miney never knew how frightened their daughter had been. She told them why she was sent home, but made light of the situation. It was over and done with, so no need to alarm her mother was Blanche's reasoning. One thing she knew for certain, if she lived to be a hundred, she'd never ever forget old Topsy.

*****

Ralph had been playing in the barn. It was just before the haying season, and the mows were nearly empty. However, there was still a sizable pile of timothy on the barn floor. Rate had been up in the mow, walking beams, swinging on hay ropes and generally enjoying himself. When he decided to leave, instead of descending the ladder as he normally would have done, he looked at the enticing pile of hay and, without hesitation, jumped from the mow. He gave a yell of pain as his right foot struck something. He looked aghast.

Oh, my God, how had that happened? The rusty tine of an old broken-handled pitchfork was stuck between the big toe and the next and protruded at least a quarter of an inch at the back of the foot near the heel. Jeepers, but it hurt! He sat and looked with dismay at the grotesque picture his foot made. Well, he'd best get busy and pull the thing out. He grabbed the broken handle and gave it a tug. It never even budged. Of course, it was rather awkward to get at, and he couldn't get much leverage.

After a few more tugs, he knew he wasn't making any progress. Sweat beaded his forehead partly from the pain and partly from the anxiety. He had to do something. He tried to stand, but that didn't work at all since it hurt more to put pressure on the foot. He couldn't hop because the handle hung down in the way. Well, he had to get to the house somehow. He hitched himself backward on his buttocks, dragging the fork and foot carefully along; thus, he went out the barn door and across the barnyard to the house. He remembered to keep looking behind him since he didn't relish the idea of sliding through a fresh cowflop or of putting his hands in one either. His progress was slow and painful. When he reached the windmill, he began to holler.

"Ma! Ma! I'm hurt! Ma, do you hear me? Help me, Ma."

"Ralph Setterington, whatever is the matter now?"

"I'm hurt, Ma. Come see."

"Oh, my land! Oh, Ralph! However did you do this? Goodness, what shall I do? Hold still now. I guess I've got to pull this thing out. It will probably hurt."

"Hurts now, so I guess it can't be worse."

Miney grasped the handle firmly, and although her face looked a little white, she began slowly and steadily to pull the tine from Rate's foot. She gave an audible gasp when it finally came free. She made no effort to stem the flow of blood.

"Good. It's bleeding. That always seems to cleanse a wound, and there is less likely to be infection or blood poisoning. I'll have to get some salt pork and something to wrap it up with. Goodness, Ralph, what were you doing?"

"I jumped out of the haymow onto a pile of hay on the barn floor. This old fork was buried under the hay, so's I couldn't see it."

"Somehow, you just attract trouble. I'm afraid that foot is going to be mighty sore for a few days. I do hope it heals all right," she said with a worried frown. "I'll be right back with some salt pork and some bandages, so you sit right here until I get back. See, it has almost stopped bleeding."

When she returned, she had a basin of hot water with her lye soap to scrub the foot, salt pork to place over the punctures, and strips of an old sheet for a bandage.

"Land's sakes, Ralph, this is going to be an awkward thing to bind up. We've got to hold the salt pork over those holes. Here, you help hold this piece in place while I get a bandage around it."

When finished, if not a professional job, it was at least a serviceable one, although somewhat cumbersome. Ralph testily put some weight on the foot and discovered that it felt much better when he didn't try to step on it. Miney helped him into the house, gave him instructions to keep off his foot as much as possible, and returned to her work in the kitchen.

She decided she didn't understand boys at all. Ralph was forever doing something dangerous. She supposed she should consider herself fortunate that thus far he had sustained no broken bones. Good thing she generally had a supply of salt pork on hand to use on his wounds. Seems like all summer long he had a piece of salt pork tied to one foot or the other. Lucky thing the salt pork drew out any poison, so no infection set in, and the punctures had always healed nicely. If he'd wear shoes, it wouldn't happen, but he could hardly wait for the first dandelion in the spring, which proclaimed it was time for small boys to doff their shoes and go barefoot until fall. He hated to put on shoes to go to church—said they made his feet burn. Millie never seemed to worry about the lad but always reiterated that boys will be boys and found all of Ralph's antics on the humorous side.

What a blessing to have had Blanche. Girls certainly were different. It seemed that Blanche could keep busy for hours doing fancy work, practicing her piano lessons—although her progress was very slow— reading, or helping with the housework. Ralph was a horse of another color. He had more energy to wear off than a young colt—always on the move, hating to sit quietly for even a short spell.

Perhaps when he got further in school, things would improve. He did love to look at books if they had any pictures in them and simple reading; sometimes, he'd even ask her what a word was, then he'd try to remember it for the next time. She was sure Millie would keep adding to his chores as he got older. Something had to be done with all that ambition he had, and if it wasn't channeled into something constructive, she just didn't know what would happen to him. Millie laughed at her fears, when he bothered to listen to her continuous complaints and observations, and merely said the boy would turn out all right.

She had to admit Ralph had been doing a good job raising the lambs. He hadn't even complained during the rest of the school year when he'd had to get up early enough to feed them before setting off for school. All seven had lived, and if Ralph put in an appearance, all seven rushed to him expecting a bottle. Now, they were fed only twice a day since there was plenty of pasture. Millie said they looked as good as the other lambs who'd been more fortunate and hadn't been disowned by their mothers. Fact was, he sounded pleased that Ralph had accepted his responsibility so readily, although he never mentioned this to Ralph.

Goodness, that brought up another problem. Mina just knew Ralph wouldn't be able to get around that well, and someone else would have to feed those lambs. Well, Millie or Jim Keenan, who'd been working for them this summer, could just see to it. After all, it was hardly work for a girl, and she knew that she wasn't about to take on the chore. It was enough that she saw to warming the milk and filling the bottles.

Wonder where Millie had found all those whiskey bottles anyhow. She supposed he had stopped by one of the saloons as they'd more than likely have a good enough supply. She didn't like to think of Millie going in one of those establishments even if it was to get empty bottles to feed the poor lambs. The neck of a whiskey bottle just fitted the nipples that the drugstore carried, and they held the right amount of milk for one feeding when the lambs were older.

Miney knew for certain John went in saloons now and again. Hadn't been too long ago that she'd overheard Cash and Millie talking about John, but she hadn't heard enough to get the whole gist of things, so she'd asked Millie later. It seemed that a couple of men had started to fight while John had been in the saloon.

Well, John had just grabbed each one by the scruff of the neck and actually picked them up so's their feet hardly touched the floor and had thrown them out the swinging doors onto the boardwalk with the admonition that they stay away until they sobered up. Hadn't made any difference that both of them had swung away trying to hit John, he had just hung on tight and walked right along like they were a couple of small boys. Of course, John stood six foot four and a half in his stocking feet, and not many men were that tall or as hefty as John since he usually tipped the scales at 280.

Miney had then asked Millie, who had told him about the incident. He'd given her this peculiar look, then admitted somewhat abashedly that he'd seen it with his own eyes. Well, that had not only surprised her, but it had also provoked her, and she had spoken her piece. Millie had hastened to explain that he had only gone in there to see his brother about some business and had left shortly after the incident. He had reminded her that Pa wouldn't like the idea of him frequenting a saloon, and not being like John, he didn't want to antagonize his father.

Mina had been more than a little upset over this admission because she felt her husband cared more about what his folks thought than what she thought. She would've liked to have told him so but, for once, bit her tongue, realizing there was no way she could change the ingrained feelings Millie had for his parents. It was a strange kind of love, built out of respect with a healthy dose of fear thrown in. Millie just never wanted to cross his father in any way. She supposed that he and John would have been better off if they could have been mixed up a little, thereby giving Millie a little more independence and letting John have a little more respect. She supposed Millie worked as hard as he did to be successful simply to please his father, looking for the words of praise, which never came.

Rate's foot remained sore for a few days even though it was healing with no sign of infection. Mina still kept it wrapped, but he hobbled around quite well and had taken over his chore of the lambs once more. Blanche still hauled his kindling for him and had been grumbling about it rather loudly the past two days. Rate thought it rather humorous and felt Blanche was getting her just due since she was gone so much enjoying herself. He really supposed he could get around well enough to do the work, but he'd hardly be the one to suggest it.

He simply aggravated Blanche all the more by sitting where he could watch her do his work. If she tried to ignore his presence, he was sure to make a big issue out of playing with Bruno, where she could hardly miss the barking dog or the loud words of praise for something well done. If not this, he merely sat on the porch and gazed idly toward the barn, whistling tunelessly when his sister came with a wagon of wood to unload. Blanche knew as well as he did that Ralph was doing this to get her goat, so she resolved not to let him know by her outward appearance that it bothered one whit. However, she promised herself that she would get even one day.

CHAPTER 5

Blanche had been asleep for some time, long enough for the first deep sleep to be finished. She stirred slightly in her bed. Something seemed to disturb her slumber. There it was again. Some thing or someone was on the porch below the north window. Whoever it was, was moving stealthily. Her throat constricted in fear. No use to look out the window. The porch roof would shield whoever was there. She was debating what to do when she heard a muffled voice.

"Miney! Miney! It's Ed. Lena needs you."

Blanche heaved a sigh of relief. She hadn't realized just how tense her muscles had been until she began to relax. She stayed very still, almost holding her breath, trying very hard to hear the muted conversation.

She knew it was Ed Clark, only she didn't quite understand just why Lena, his wife, needed her mother in the middle of the night. She wondered if Ma was going to get dressed and go with him. Try as she might, she could hear no further conversation. Stealthily, she slipped out of bed and hovered by the open door leading onto the east porch roof. There was enough moonlight, so she could easily see the road. Sure enough, there stood Ed's buggy with his old driving mare tied to a tree. Next, she saw Ed and Mina emerge from the shadows of the porch, get into the buggy, and leave. Blanche was completely baffled. She looked in to see if

Ralph had heard anything, but he was sound asleep, so no use to rouse him.

There were many things lately that puzzled Blanche a great deal. A few months ago when her monthlies had started, she had been greatly upset and had asked Ma why this was happening, wanting some kind of reassurance from her mother that she was simply a normal girl. Ma had acted rather embarrassed, and the only explanation she had given was that it was something a woman had to contend with every month. Blanche had not been satisfied with this meager bit of information, although any further attempts to discuss it had met with failure. Miney had merely indicated that when Blanche was older, she would understand, but until then, this scant bit of information would have to suffice.

Just like Blanche had been noticing that whenever any children or young girls came into the Ladies Missionary Society meetings, all talk stopped immediately. She, Fern, and Hazel had stood outside the door one day trying to hear what was being said, only the blamed door had been too thick, or the women had been talking too softly, because all they could get was the steady hum of voices. However, when they had burst in rather unceremoniously, all conversation halted, and some of the women looked ill at ease. Blanche had questioned her mother about this.

"Ma, what do women talk about at Ladies Missionary Society?"

"Oh, recipes, sewing, kids' ailments."

"Then, if that is all, why does everyone stop talking when we girls come in? Ralph says it was like that one day when he came by to ask you something. Just what is being said that we can't hear?" she demanded.

"Why—why, nothing," replied a flustered Miney. "It wasn't intentional, I'm sure. We just wanted to give you girls a chance to say what you'd come to say."

Blanche had realized her mother was putting her off, not giving the real reason. The girls had figured out that it must have something to do with being wives and mothers. That was another thing—no one seemed to know where babies came from.

Everyone knew that a woman had to get married first, but none of the girls knew why. Blanche would have liked to have questioned her mother about this, only she realized Miney would not discuss such a topic.

Blanche finally drifted back to sleep although it was somewhat troubled and beset by weird dreams.

"Blanche! Time to get up."

That was Pa's voice. She wondered sleepily why he, instead of her mother, was calling her.

"Yes, Pa," came the drowsy answer.

She dressed quickly and came down the stairs. She noted that Rate was ahead of her, having had his share of chores to do before breakfast.

"Where's Ma?" asked Blanche, looking around.

"She's at Clark's. Think you can rustle us up some vittles? I've got the fire going."

"I suppose so, Pa. But why isn't Ma here?"

"Because she isn't."

Blanche knew better than to press the matter further when Pa took that tone of voice. She went to the kitchen to begin breakfast. Pa had followed her.

"Here, Blanche, I'll slice the side pork."

"Thank you, Pa. I'll get the bread cut. Do you want eggs too?" She had already put the coffeepot on to boil.

"Reckon I do. Man can't work on an empty stomach, you know."

All the while Blanche was getting breakfast, her mind was in a turmoil. Her actions were mechanical as she removed the cheesecloth from the table, set the plates in place, put on the jelly and butter, in between turning the strips of fat side pork in the pan. When the meat was done, she removed it to a plate that she promptly put in the warming oven above the stove top; she fried the eggs in the deep grease from the meat. Millie noted the meat with satisfaction—fat meat was his favorite, and the side pork had only a thin vein of lean.

Why hadn't Ma come home? Rate managed to ask Blanche if she knew why Ma had gone to Clark's, and she just shook her head.

Breakfast was over before Mina returned home. She looked plumb tuckered out, and her funny hip was sticking out, so she walked haltingly and with pain.

"Ma, where have you been?" demanded Blanche.

"Up to Clark's. Didn't your pa tell you that?"

"Why did you have to go there?"

Blanche's voice was petulant.

"Lena needed me."

"What for? Is she sick?"

"Not exactly."

Mina carefully lowered herself into a chair. My, but it had been a demanding and tiring night. She'd have liked to go to bed, only there was work to be done.

"If she isn't sick, why did Ed come get you?" persisted Blanche.

"When you're older, you'll understand," said Miney.

"Blanche, quit pestering your mother. Can't you see that she's tuckered out?" put in Millie.

Blanche shut her mouth in a tight line. She'd not ask another question, but she'd not do any more work than what she absolutely had to for the rest of the day. Much she cared if Ma's hip hurt. If that's the way they wanted to treat her, like some small child—well, let them. She had intended to do the sweeping after she finished dishes, only now she wasn't so sure. She supposed if Ma asked her, she would, but otherwise, she would just conveniently forget. Her stubborn English heritage once more took over.

A few days later, Blanche learned that the Clarks had a new baby boy, born the night of June 16, whom they named Milford after her own father. Somehow, Blanche tied together the two facts—her mother's absence and the new baby. Now, why couldn't her mother have given her just a simple explanation instead of being so secretive? Blanche felt guilty that she had used her mother so badly, but there were times when Ma just left her feeling frustrated because there were things she didn't understand, and where else was she to get the answers if not from her own mother?

Ralph had been getting around quite well for several days; in fact, his foot was almost back to normal. At the dinner table, Millie spoke to his son.

"Rate, there's a patch of bull thistles in the cornfield that need hoeing. That would be a good job for you this afternoon."

"Can I have Curly and Burl come help me?"

"I think not."

"But, Pa, I've helped them with their chores afore this, so it'd be only fair if they came to help me. Besides, we could get the job done lots quicker," he added hopefully.

"Rate, I know boys. One boy is fine, two boys are half a boy, and three boys are no boy at all."

Rate opened his mouth to ask his father what he meant, but the look on his father's face told him the question was settled. Blanche kicked him under the table and gave him a sweet little grin, which really meant she was laughing at him. His mother seemed lost in thought and had paid no attention to the verbal exchange between father and son. It was not the last time Ralph was to hear his father express these sentiments, and while not fully understood at first, in time, he came to agree that Pa's idea was not completely far-fetched.

Bruno was Rate's only companion that afternoon, and Ralph was more than a little miffed at the dog because Bruno had wanted to follow Millie instead of him. He concluded that dogs were not always the loyal friend they were supposed to be. Actually, he knew that Bruno preferred Pa to himself, and yet, Pa never paid him that much mind, so why the dog liked him best was hard to figger out. 'Course, he must admit that when he and Pa got to scuffling, which happened rather often, Bruno always took his part and was likely to give Pa a little nip. Sometimes, when Bruno nipped a little too hard, Rate thought it made Pa more than a trifle mad, but Pa never said much, and Bruno was pretty darn clever about dodging any blow directed at him.

Thinking of wrestling with his father brought a smile to Ralph's lips. He wondered if there would ever be a time when he'd be able to best Pa. As it was now, no matter how much by surprise he took Millie, Ralph was always the one to come out on the short end. Still, it was fun to try. There were times when Pa sure was fun. Guess he was lucky to have such a good father even if it did include hoeing thistles from a cornfield with no help from his friends.

"Blanche, where's Pa and Ma going?"

"Weren't you listening? Don't be such a dunce."

"I heard them say Nigra Falls, but what's that?"

"It's Ni-ag-ara Falls, and it is a big waterfall by Canada. They are also going to the exposition."

"Is that all? What they going there for?"

"Why would anyone go anyplace? To see something. Brothers. I wonder if they are all as dumb as you. Ma and Pa are just taking a trip for enjoyment. The exposition is like a big fair, I guess. I think Niagara Falls isn't too far from where Pa was born. You do know that Pa was born in Canada and that Grandfather and our great-grandfather came here when Pa was two years old."

"I guess I know that. Leastways I've heard Grandfather talk about his home in Canada afore now, but I don't really know if it's far or not."

"Well, it's a lot farther than we've ever been from home."

"What are they doing with us?"

"Aunt Lorin said we could stay with her and Uncle Norman. I don't really like Aunt Lorin all that much. She's sort of odd if you ask me. I suppose I can put up with her for a few days."

Ralph pondered the situation. He had never been away from both parents before. Of course, he had spent a day or an afternoon with Grandmother, Aunt Lorin, or Grandma Smith all by himself. He was glad they were to stay with Aunt Lorin since he liked her, and she liked him. He guessed Pa wouldn't want to be gone very long 'cause he'd heard Pa say something about this was the only time they'd have before it was time to start putting up hay, and time would be short.

Mina and Millie, along with Clayton Sherman and his wife, left on Thursday from the depot in Elsie. Rate was sad to see his parents leave, but Ma had actually hugged and kissed him goodbye, and Pa had given him a bear hug and whispered that he'd bring back something special.

The days with Aunt Lorin passed pleasantly and quickly. Rate enjoyed the coddling from Aunt Lorin. She took him to the store twice and gave him a whole nickel each time to buy any kind of candy he wanted. Ma was never this generous. True, he'd had a difficult time deciding just what he wanted, but it sure had been fun. Aunt Lorin made awful good cookies too, and she wasn't near as fussy about how many he ate as Ma was.

When Millie and Mina returned, they picked up the children from Lorin's and hastened on home. Millie was anxious to get back to work. He was not a man to enjoy being idle for many days, so he was more than ready to get back in harness.

Ralph feared to bring up what was foremost on his mind: what had Pa brought him, or had he forgotten?

When Miney unpacked the valises, she brought out a paperweight and a beaded pincushion. Now, the paperweight was of plain, heavy glass with a browntone picture of the falls under the domed top. However, the pincushion was made of several kinds and sizes of brilliantly colored beads over a beautiful blue-gray satin. The beaded words read "From Niagara Falls." Rate didn't realize it was a pincushion, a girl's gift, so he thought it was beautiful. He was sure this must be the something special Pa had promised. Then, he realized Ma was speaking.

"Blanche, this pincushion is for you, and Ralph, yours is the paperweight."

"Oh, Ma, it's—it's—why, it's just gorgeous."

With that, Blanche threw her arms around her mother and kissed her in an unaccustomed display of affection.

"Thank you, Ma. I just love it."

"Ralph, you haven't said a thing," observed Miney.

"Thank you, Ma. It's nice."

"Don't you like the paperweight, Ralph?"

"Sure, Ma, it's fine. I like it."

If his voice faltered a little at the tiny white lie, Miney never noticed.

She had already turned back to her unpacking.

Ralph was to learn that this was only the beginning; he would always come out second best, Blanche would always come first in everything. A bitter pill for one so young to swallow, yet neither Miney nor Millie would ever have admitted to anyone, much less themselves, that this partiality ever existed in any form. Perhaps they couldn't see the forest for the trees and, therefore, never realized they were being so very prejudicial. It was a very disillusioned and saddened small boy who went to bed that night. What had happened to Pa's promise for something special? He really couldn't see anything so special about the paperweight they had given him; still, they had brought something, so he guessed he should be pleased.

"Blanche, I'm a man short today, so you get to drive the team on the hay rope."

"Millie, do you think she can?"

"She's done it once or twice before. You just never knew about it."

"Well! It's not a woman's work, you know."

"Miney, just keep still. Blanche, I want you out to the barn when we come up with the first wagon."

"All right, Pa. But if I'm to drive that team, you are not to load the forks too heavy. If you do, I'll quit."

Ralph stared. Pa was letting Blanche get away with sassing him. Bet Pa would never let him talk like that.

"What do you mean?"

"Just what I said. Sometimes, you push those forks in so deep, the team can hardly pull them up. I'll not make them work so hard. You just never consider those poor horses. Now, promise me, Pa."

"All right, Blanche. We'll load light so the team won't be overworked." Millie chuckled. Golly, but when she was like that, she sure did put him in mind of Ma. The tilt of her head, the way her eyes flashed, and the set of her mouth. He supposed he shouldn't let her talk to him in that tone of voice, and if it wasn't that she even sounded like Ma, he supposed he wouldn't have tolerated it.

The hay was forked onto a wagon in the fields, then brought to the barn. Here an inverted U-shaped hayfork, which was over three feet high with a spread of thirty inches or more, was lowered by means of a heavy rope from the car on a track fastened to the center of the barn roof; the other end of the rope passed through a pulley at the north side of the barn door and was fastened to the eveners where a team of horses was hitched. Each side of the fork had a finger that slid up out of the way as the fork was shoved into the hay on the wagon, then the finger was pushed out by a lever at the top of the fork and locked into place. If the hay was long and piled well on the wagon, when the horses were driven away from the barn, the fork rose with a large bunch of hay attached. When it rose high enough to clear the beams into the haymow, the team was halted; the car locked the fork in place automatically, and it was drawn over into the mow by another smaller rope and pulley series. A trip rope hanging from the lever locking the fingers was jerked, retracting the fingers and dumping the load of hay.

All this was if everything worked satisfactorily. Sometimes, when the hay was short, it did not cling together well enough, and some of it fell from the fork back onto the wagon. Once in a while, the trip rope got tangled up and couldn't be found, or if found, it failed to trip the forks. Sometimes, if a farmer didn't keep close watch of the ropes being used, a rope broke. All work had to stop until the two pieces of rope were once more spliced together.

All had been going well, and Blanche had been satisfied with the way Millie was loading the forks—until the last, small load.

Millie set the forks, and Blanche dutifully drove the team until Millie hollered "Whoa!" That load of hay was dumped in the mow, and the forks returned to be drawn down to the wagon rack to be set once again.

This time, Blanche had driven the team only about half the usual distance when she heard Millie holler.

"Blanche! Stop the horses!"

"Whoa! Whoa, there."

The team stopped as she pulled back on the lines.

"What's wrong, Pa?"

Blanche turned to look back to the barn and saw that not only was there hay clinging to the forks, but Millie had shoved them down so hard the pointed legs had stuck in the wagon rack, and that was going up along with the hay.

"Pa! Just look what you've done."

Blanche dropped the lines and ran to the barn.

"I thought I told you not to load heavy so's old Mage and Jen wouldn't have to work so hard. Now, look what you've gone and done. That rack is heavier than the hay. I'm done, Pa. I'm not going to drive no more. I told you I wouldn't if you didn't have some consideration for the team. I meant just what I said. Besides, it isn't a woman's work."

With a toss of her head, Blanche flounced off to the house. Millie gave Jim a sheepish grin.

"Sure riled her good, didn't I? Gets more like Ma everyday. Guess if this wasn't the last load, I'd have to change her mind for her. As it is, no harm's done. One thing about Blanche, when she makes up her mind to something, she's powerful hard to dissuade. Pity the poor man she's to marry."

"Your mother found one to match her. Leastways, I never felt your father couldn't hold his own. Maybe Blanche will do as well," said Jim.

"Could be. Guess we'd better get this mess straightened out afore the team gets tired of standing. Rate, you grab those lines and just hold 'em steady so they won't start walking off."

"All right, Pa. Can I finish drivin' 'em when you're ready?"

"We'll see."

Boy, Blanche sure had talked up to Pa. Bet if he ever tried it, Pa would trounce him to within an inch of his life. Wonder why

Pa always seemed to let Blanche do as she pleased. Fact was, he always seemed to think it comical the way he chuckled. Maybe it was because she reminded him of his mother, and everyone knew that Pa had never spoken up to his mother in all his years. Must be that was the reason.

Blanche never liked to be told she resembled Grandmother Setterington. Guess she was just too stubborn to admit the resemblance. Blanche had told him once that in no way did she ever want to be anything like Grandmother. Still, Pa was always saying blood will tell, so he supposed she just couldn't help herself.

Miney had thought Blanche seemed rather quiet at dinner. She was the one who usually had something to say, and if Millie was to do much talking during a meal, it would be in response to some query from his daughter. However, today's meal had been a quiet one, and even doing the dishes afterward had been an unusually quiet occasion. Mina tried to draw Blanche into conversation, but her efforts were to no avail. Blanche remained quiet and morose, much unlike her usual self.

Work finished, she went upstairs to her room with no word of explanation. Millie left for town, taking Ralph with him, so Miney was left to herself as she sat on the porch to do some of the seemingly endless mending. July 26, her birthday. She doubted if the children even thought of it, and she knew Millie would never remember anything so trivial. Well, it didn't matter much. So she was a year older. Didn't make her feel any different.

She finished putting the hem in a dress for Blanche. The girl had grown taller so fast that the skirt had been too short. Why, it had been more than midway to her knees, showing over two inches of calf above the shoes. Well, now it was done. She supposed she should have made Blanche do her own sewing since she was getting to be such a young lady. However, she could most certainly finish the chore much more quickly than her daughter.

Dress in hand, Miney stepped to the stairway, opened the door, and called, "Blanche. Ma's got your dress finished. Come take care of it."

"Yes, Ma," came the rather muffled reply.

When Blanche reached the bottom of the steps and extended her hand for the dress, she kept her eyes downcast. Miney looked at her critically.

"Blanche, have you been crying?"

"Not…not much."

"Come here. Let me look at you. Why, child, your pretty eyes are all red. What is the matter? Aren't you feeling well?"

Miney took her daughter's chin in her hand and tilted Blanche's head back so she could see the girl's tearstained face, clearly noting the reddened, swollen eyes.

"Yes, Ma. I feel all right. I'm not sick."

"Then, why have you been crying? If you tell me, perhaps I can help. Don't you want to tell Ma?"

"Oh, Ma. It's just—it's just that I know what today is."

"Well, what is it?" came the baffled question.

"It's your birthday," she wailed.

"I've known that all day, but I don't see why that should make you cry."

"But, Ma, you're thirty-five today," blurted out Blanche. And with that, she burst into tears anew.

Miney began to laugh. "Child, child, child. Whatever makes you cry because I'm thirty-five?"

"But, Ma, it's so old, and I don't want to lose you."

Miney took the sobbing girl into her arms, dress and all.

"Sweetheart, Ma's not going to leave you. Thirty-five may sound old to you, but Ma isn't exactly ancient, you know. Don't you remember that Grandma was seventy-six, and that is more than twice my age. Blanche, is that what has been ailing you all day?"

"I guess so. Ma, I love you so much, and I just thought that you were getting so old, and however would I get along without you?"

"You silly little goose." Miney laughed. "Ma loves you too, and I'm not as over the hill as you think." Miney kissed her daughter noisily. "There. Give Ma a smile. You are so pretty when you smile. Go wash your eyes with cold water. The redness spoils their looks, and you do have such beautiful eyes. In fact, to Ma, you are a mighty charming and pretty young girl. 'Course anyone who's as old as I am certainly isn't much of a judge." Miney laughed.

"Ma, you're just teasing. Here, I'll take care of my dress. Thank you for fixing it. I guess I'll have to start doing these things for myself. Grandmother says I must learn to be independent," she announced as she went back up the stairs.

Fine thing for Lovina to tell a young girl when if Mother Setterington had her way, everyone would be dependent on her. Why, she hadn't thought Miney knew enough to buy Blanche's clothes when the girl had started school. Mina had made Blanche's dresses that first year, and Lovina had looked haughtily down her nose and asked if that was what she intended Blanche to wear to school. Miney had said that she thought Blanche would be dressed as well as the other girls; then, Lovina reiterated that she doubted if the Wooley girls or the Albaughs or any of the Bates children wore homemade dresses except for every day—or perhaps when they hired a competent seamstress to do something special. This had hurt Miney's feelings deeply, and she had felt quite taken down because she had put forth a lot of effort on those dresses.

Lorin, who often supplemented Norm's income and as a young woman had even earned her living as a dressmaker, had helped her with the more fancy of the three. Well, Mother Setterington had informed her that since she had already gone to the time and effort she, Lovina, supposed it would have to suffice for this year. "However, next year I will take her to Owosso to Christian's and buy her something which *I* find more suitable. Please keep that in mind," she had said in her most dictatorial manner.

Mina had wished the floor would open up and let her drop right out of Mother Setterington's sight and life. Of course, it hadn't happened, but true to her word, the next year, Mother had taken Blanche on the train to Owosso and bought Blanche not three, but four dresses and had presented them with the bill. Miney supposed she should have been grateful that Mother had paid the train fare and that Mother had only bought material for the new petticoats and pantaloons, not ready-made ones. However, Miney had been put out at the expense—she could have made the dresses for half the price, but Millie had made no objection and had shelled out the money without batting an eyelash. Miney had expected at least some kind of remark, but no, Millie still jumped whenever his mother snapped her fingers.

Last year, Blanche had raised her objections by asking why Grandmother always had to take her shopping because she would rather go with Ma. Miney was at loss as to what to say, so she had told Blanche to ask her father. Millie merely retorted, "Because that's what your grandmother wants." Even Blanche hadn't said more, knowing that her father would tolerate no criticism of his mother by his daughter. Blanche had told her mother that she wouldn't mind so much if only her grandmother would let her choose at least one dress herself. As it was, Lovina had her try on several and then told the saleslady which ones they would take, without even asking for Blanche's opinion. Blanche wanted to rebel, but she knew it would do no good. If Pa and Ma couldn't stand up to Lovina Setterington, how could she? Still, there might come a day.

Ruby had been visiting her mother and father for a few days. She and Lovina drove out to the farm one evening to visit Millie and his family. While there, it was decided that Blanche and Ralph would go home with her for the next week. Both children seemed enthused over the prospects of a trip to Big Rapids.

Perhaps Ralph was a little reluctant although he said nothing. He thought his aunt Ruby had changed a great deal since she was married. While they lived in St. Johns, she seemed much the same. 'Course Uncle Mac had only been a rather lowly paid bookkeeper for Masons. Now that he had a position in the bank in Big Rapids, Aunt Ruby put on airs. She had a seamstress come in to make her dresses. Grandmother probably paid for them, he thought maliciously. Anyway, she felt she had to dress the part as the wife of a bank employee who was certain to go up in the world.

Rate thought she rather looked down her nose at Ma and Pa thinking she and Uncle Mac were better than simple farm folk. Oh, well, she treated him pretty good and really never favored Blanche like the others did. Anyway, it would be a nice trip.

Rate hadn't figured on getting bored because he had no one to play with. A boy could only do so much to entertain himself during the day. 'Course, one day wasn't so bad as they had gone down to the Muskegon River and had taken a picnic lunch. Aunt Ruby was a good cook—no disputing that. She always let him have two pieces of pie, when Ma sometimes said one was enough. Anyway, they'd had fun. Uncle Mac had even played catch with him.

Another day turned out to be exciting. Aunt Ruby called to him where he was playing in the backyard.

"Ralph, the lawn needs watering. Do you think you can manage to water it? Here, hold the hose at an angle so it sprays like falling rain. That's it. Now, do along the sides and the front too."

"All right, Aunt Ruby. I'll do a good job, you'll see."

"I'm sure you will."

Ruby went back into the house to do her morning work. Blanche was doing the dusting, so there wasn't much to do. It was going to be a hot one, and so far, no breeze to help. The curtains hung limp at the open windows.

"Aunt Ruby! Aunt Ruby, come quick," cried Blanche from the parlor. Ruby hastened to where her niece stood staring at the double windows. Water was coming in, thoroughly soaking the curtains, wetting the couch and the rug. Apparently, Blanche was so surprised, she did not realize the cause.

"Rate! Rate!" screamed Ruby. "You turn that hose away from the house this instant. Rate! Do you hear?"

"Yes, Aunt Ruby. I hear you. What's wrong?"

"You were spraying water into the house. That's what was wrong."

"Gosh, I didn't mean to. I was watering the bushes," he explained.

"But those bushes are in front of the windows, and the windows are open. Oh, Rate, my curtains will have to be washed, and it is going to take the rug a while to dry."

"I'm sorry, honest, I am."

"I know," sighed Ruby. "Go on and finish your job, but stick to watering the grass, not bushes."

"Boys!" came from Blanche. "Aunt Ruby, he just always gets into trouble. I'll get the mop and soak up what water I can."

"Thank you, Blanche. I'll get the curtains down and get them washed."

Washing curtains, while not difficult, was a time-consuming job. They had to be lightly starched and put on curtain stretchers until they dried. Next, they were sprinkled, rolled in a towel until slightly damp, and then ironed, being careful not to stretch them out of shape. It was not a job Ruby liked. But like it or not, it had to be done. She had always rather suspicioned that Mina and Mother exaggerated the stories of the mischief Ralph got into, only now she wasn't so sure. Still, the lad had meant no harm, and he was such a good-looking child. In fact, she felt that both of Millie's children were exceptionally good-looking. She would consider herself lucky if she and Oliver were ever blessed with children, to have them as nice-looking.

*****

"Rate, go down the road and fetch Jen from where I tied her in the fencerow this morning."

"All right, Pa."

"Don't dawdle. Supper is near ready."

"Yes, Pa."

Boy, when Pa wanted something done, he expected it done right now. What made him think it would take so long anyhow? 'Course, she was tied clear down to the line fence, but that wasn't so far.

Ralph hurried along to the black mare who stood contentedly by the roadside fence. Apparently, she had had a good feast since the grass was nibbled short as far as the rope would let her move.

"Jen, just you hold still while I get on your back. No need for me to walk back when I can ride you."

He maneuvered the horse next to the rail fence and slid over onto her back. He grabbed a handful of mane and kicked her ribs with his bare heels.

"C'mon, Jen. Let's go."

The mare ambled off at a slow walk, but the nearer she got to the barn, the faster she went, and Ralph was intent on the task of staying on her broad back. Just as she turned into the north driveway, *whomp!* Something struck his forehead, and off he slid. Wow! His head hurt something awful. He put his hand to his forehead, drew it away, looked at it tentatively, half expecting it to be covered with blood. It wasn't. Dumb horse. She'd turned too close to the oak tree, and he'd been caught by a lowhanging limb. His head throbbed.

Better put the fool mare into the barn. At least she hadn't run off, just stood patiently waiting in front of the barn door for someone to put her in the barn.

Ralph hurried to finish his job and get to the house so he wouldn't be late for supper. Neither Miney nor Millie tolerated tardiness at mealtime. He hastily washed and had slid into his chair before his mother looked at him.

"Whatever happened to you? Why, Ralph, your forehead is scratched and—here, let me look at it—you've got a bump as large as an egg. Millie, just look at this."

"I'm lookin', Miney. Well, Rate, want to explain?"

"Gosh, Pa, I hit my head on that low limb on the oak tree. Jen was comin' faster than I wanted, so I was workin' at stayin' on, and she cut too close to the tree. See if I ever ride a horse again."

"If you could ride well, you'd have had your horse under control and wouldn't have let her turn so short towards the tree," observed Blanche.

Ralph wrinkled up his nose at his sister. "Like to see you do any better," he muttered.

"That's enough," said Millie, then added, "How's the head feel?"

"Sore. And it aches."

"My land, Ralph, must you always get hurt?"

"Honest, Ma, I didn't do it on purpose."

"I should think not. I just wish you would learn to be more careful. After you eat, a cold cloth on your forehead might make your head feel better."

"Miney, quit fussin'. The lad's no sissy and can take a little bump. Can't you, Rate?"

Lot Pa knew. It wasn't his head that hurt. At least Ma had showed some concern, but then, mothers were like that, he guessed.

A few days later, Millie came into the kitchen from the windmill door, then continued into the dining room. He looked somber.

Miney looked up from her crocheting. "Millie, whatever is the matter?"

"Didn't you notice any of the fracas up at Clayt's?" he countered.

"Now that you mention it, I did notice three or four buggies in the yard. What was going on?"

"Young Ed just died."

"Ed Sherman, Clayt's nephew?"

"That's right, Miney. He's only about thirteen or fourteen."

"For land's sake, what happened?"

"Seems he was giving Burl a ride on the handlebars of his bicycle. They were down the Ridge a piece when a rig came along, and the boys had to get out of the way. Well, they brushed into some bushes, and Burl got his heel caught in the spokes, jerked the handlebars out of Ed's hand, and tipped them over. Ed got that handlebar right in the pit of the stomach when they fell. He just lay there doubled up in pain. Burl's heel was bleedin' pretty good, but he started for Clayt's yellin' his head off. The man in the rig stopped, Clayt came runnin' out, and they both got back to where Ed lay. The two of them picked Ed up and carried him into the house. First they called Ed's folks, then they called the doctor. Guess his ma got there just before he died. Anyway, the doctor no more'n got there when he up and died."

"How awful."

"I happened along about then. Wondered why all the rigs so stopped to see what was wrong. Felt sorry for Burl. He said it was all his fault because he was the one who made them tip over. The kid had quite a cut on his heel, so the doctor took a couple of stitches. Guy tried to tell Burl it was just an accident, but the boy just cries and says he should have kept his feet away from the spokes."

"Poor child. Those boys have always been close, more so than some cousins."

"I know. Guess it was just meant to be. 'Course it was a dumb thing to give the boy a ride on the handlebars, but kids often do that. I'd better get my team put away. Where's Rate? He should be told."

"I don't know, but he's likely not far."

"You want to do the tellin'?"

"Suppose I can. If you find him, send him in. He'll feel pretty badly— him being so close to the Sherman boys."

Millie nodded his head in agreement.

Miney was the one who explained to Ralph what had happened. He hadn't said much, there wasn't much one could say. Rate wondered why one so young had to die. Poor Burl. It was sort of his fault, but then, if the rig hadn't come along—if, if, if. God sure had strange ways of running the world, and Rate guessed he would never understand why certain things happened, they just did.

Usually, Blanche began looking forward to school starting along about the middle of August. This year was different. The nearer the time came, the more she dreaded it; the reason was that this year she would be entering the seventh grade. This meant she would no longer be in one of the downstairs classrooms but would have to go to the second floor. It also meant she would have Miss Finch. What a horrible thought. For the past two years, she had heard many stories about how strict Miss Finch was and how she ruled the classroom with an iron hand. Why, it was said she even used a razor strap on the students for just any little infraction of the rules, which everyone knew were so outlandish it was just impossible not to break one once in a while. The thought of being in such an environment terrified Blanche.

The day of doom grew steadily closer. Blanche even considered faking some sort of illness just to put off the awful day a little while longer. Then, she thought of some of her mother's homemade remedies and changed her mind.

If Miney thought her daughter was less than exuberant about the beginning of the school term, she said nothing. She realized it would do no good to question her daughter because if Blanche did not want to share her thoughts, no amount of coaxing would entice her to divulge what she was thinking.

Miney need not have been concerned. Blanche came home from school on Friday night chattering like a magpie. It was Miss Finch this and Miss Finch that, and how she was looking forward to the school year.

"I thought Miss Finch was so strict no one liked her."

"Oh, no, Ma. She's just the nicest teacher. She says the funniest things without cracking a smile, but her eyes always laugh. Fern and I always ask if we can do things for her like erase boards and such."

Miney laughed. "See all that worrying you did for naught."

"I guess so. But she's not one bit like what we'd heard. 'Course, no one did anything wrong yet. I guess probably she wouldn't tolerate anyone fooling around. She expects work done on time. She is such an interesting person. I never liked history all that much, but she sure makes it fun to learn."

Blanche had made the observation that many a student was to make: Kate Finch was a demanding teacher, but an interesting one, and one who managed to reach each student who passed through her classroom—a truly dedicated teacher, devoted to the only children she was ever to have, for she never married.

Wheat had been a good money crop the past two years—almost as good as hay. While Millie was busy dragging a field for the crop of winter wheat he would soon sow, Miney waited for Ralph to come home from school so they could drive to town. The main reason was to get Blanche from her grandmother's, but if Mina went to town, she could always think of something she needed from the store.

Rate often wondered just why his mother always had to have him go along when she still considered him enough of a child that she had to drive instead of him. Mothers could be so blamed hard to figger out at times; now, Pa often let him drive knowing that a boy almost eight could handle a horse right well. Pa even let him drive by himself although he knew Ma often berated his father for this. 'Course, Pa was kind of careful which horse he gave him to drive since some of Pa's horses weren't exactly trustworthy. Anyway, Mina was driving Old Mikey today, and they pulled up to the hitching rail in front of Van Deusen's General Store.

Mina took her time about getting down from the buggy while Rate scrambled down in a hurry and tethered the horse securely—not that Old Mikey needed tying, he'd have stood there till doom's day, lessen someone came along and picked up the lines. Ralph waited, but just as Miney stepped down onto the boardwalk—the refuse from the multitude of horses over the years had resulted in the street being some six inches higher than the boardwalk—a young man accosted Miney, making unintelligible sounds, his arms waving and his fingers moving excitedly.

"Dummy" Harris was deaf and dumb. Rate knew his given name was Edgar, only everyone just called him Dummy. It was not the first time Ralph had seen his mother use her hands and fingers to "talk" to Dummy. Rate often marveled that they could carry on a conversation this way. Of course, since Mina was one of the few people other than his own family who could talk to him, and since she always treated him kindly, Dummy almost worshiped her. Rate could sense there was something urgent in what was being said.

The sign language flew, then Miney gasped, "Oh, no! Ralph, Edgar says that someone has shot President McKinley. Oh my goodness."

"How does he know?"

"He was down to the depot, and it came over the telegraph not long ago. Edgar can read, you know, and he saw the message. We'd best hurry with our purchases and get back home to tell your father."

"Is he dead?"

"Your father? Oh, you mean the president. No. Leastways not yet. Edgar said they didn't know much about it except he's been shot. I knew the president was to be at the Pan-American Exposition at Buffalo. Some man just up and shot him. Had the gun bandaged up in his hand like he had something wrong with his hand. Why would anyone want to kill the president of the United States?"

Rate pondered the question. Why would anyone want to kill anybody whether they was president or not? Grown folks were hard to understand, that was for certain. Ralph hoped they would sentence the man to death. Didn't the Bible say an eye for an eye?

Dummy Harris had been right in his information. On Friday, September 6, 1901, Leon Czolgosz, an anarchist, had shot President William McKinley; the president was still alive, and the wound was not thought to be critical. He had been taken to a hospital in Buffalo, and the doctors were rather optimistic. Then, his condition abruptly worsened. Vice President Roosevelt was on standby while a whole nation waited for the news each day. Special services of prayer for his recovery were held at churches all over this vast country; the Elsie Baptist Church was among them.

On September 14, the president succumbed to gangrene, and the nation set about to mourn a president. On the afternoon of the same day, Theodore Roosevelt took the oath of office; no nation can remain without a leader at the helm even though they lament the passing of a competent man.

Millie was optimistic. Hadn't McKinley chosen Roosevelt for his running mate? Well, then, the man must think along the same lines. Millie was not concerned with a foreign policy, he wanted only a good domestic trade with farmers earning a fair price for their various crops. Millie did not care for newfangled notions in the way of automobiles, nor could he envision farming being done by anything other than good draft horses and a reliable man.

Milford had always been a skeptic about something new; the old, if it worked well, would suffice. Machinery to save time was only for men who were lazy, and he was not to be counted in their number. Thus, while he felt saddened that a man had lost his life in so brutal a fashion, he felt no qualms about the twenty-sixth president doing a comparable job.

The schoolyard buzzed with talk of the assassination. The older boys made their boasts as to how they would have handled the situation. The younger ones, Ralph included, were awed by the event. Since to them, President McKinley had been only a man whom they had seen in pictures, they felt no personal loss or tragedy. So a president had died—the country still had a president, and life continued in the same manner as before. The guilty man should be punished because he had broken one of God's Commandments, nothing more, nothing less; to the very young, it was all exceedingly simple.

All summer the Detroit Bridge and Iron Works had been working on a new metal bridge across the Maple River by the gristmill. The old wooden structure had been deemed unsafe, especially after the near disaster of last spring's record high water. The new bridge was directly to the east of the wooden structure; men and horses were still hauling and leveling gravel since only the approaches were unfinished. Ralph had already walked across the new bridge. It was much higher above the water than the old one, and the sides were open. Rate had kept pretty much to the center since it was sort of scary being in the open with the water so far below; he kept expecting the bridge to wiggle, but it didn't. The planking on the old one really rattled when any vehicle passed over it; he was sure this one was going to be virtually soundless.

When the bridge was finally completed, the old landmark was torn down with only the pilings still standing like sentinels in the water, mute testimony that the bridge had once existed. At each end of the new bridge was a prominently displayed sign: Ten Dollars fine for riding or driving faster than a walk.

CHAPTER 6

Ralph and Don (Curly) Sherman were discussing a
grievance at noon hour.

"Rate, it ain't fair that the older boys get to get out of
school to bring the water."

"Maybe so. Only I don't think we could carry a full pail all
that way." Stafford School did not have a well. There was a flowing
well on the east side of the road by the bridge across from where
the Naegle family lived, and the older boys took turns carrying a
pail at a time from there. It usually took two pails to last the day,
one for the morning and one for the afternoon. The pail set on a
stand just inside the door at the back of the schoolroom, and the
children drank from a single dipper.

"Maybe by ourself we couldn't," Don agreed. "How about if
she let us go together? We could either take turns or we could
carry the pail between us."

"Suppose we could at that."

"Whyn't you ask?"

"Not me. It was your idea."

"Aw, Rate, you know she's more likely to say yes if you ask."

"That's not so."

"She likes you better'n she does me."

"Naw, she doesn't. She just got mad the other day 'cause you
were fighting."

"That's what I mean. She ain't mad at you."

"What about how she hollered when I stuck both of Alice's pigtails in my inkwell?" asked Rate with a mischievous grin.

"I'd forgotten that. Maybe I should ask."

"I'll go with you, but you do the talking."

Ralph and Don went back into the one-room schoolhouse and approached Miss Peabody's desk situated off to the southwest side of the front of the room. They paused in front of her desk not knowing if they should interrupt her since she was correcting some arithmetic papers.

Looking up, she asked, "Do you boys want something?"

"Yes, Miss Peabody. Me and Rate—uh, Ralph, here, we want to know if we can get the water for this afternoon."

"Oh, Don, do you think you can carry it so far? You know it is quite a ways."

"Yessum. That's why both of us want to go."

"You know neither of you is very big. I'm just not sure you could manage. A pail of water can get pretty heavy."

"We know, ma'am, but we can do it. Honest. Just you give us a try. We're stronger than we look, ain't we, Rate?"

"I sometimes carry water for chickens and such at home," volunteered Rate. "Can we try? Please?"

"All right. You'll have to leave now so you will be back in time for your afternoon reading class."

"Oh, boy. Let's go. C'mon, Rate."

Rate carefully set the dipper aside while Don grabbed the pail. They set off with a vim down the schoolyard hill and into the road.

"Race you there," shouted Curly as he took off running.

Rate ran to catch him. Panting a little, he said, "There's no use to hurry. Reading class don't start when the bell rings, so we've got plenty of time."

"Guess you're right," admitted Don.

They slowed their steps, and Rate took his turn carrying the pail.

Upon reaching the bridge, they crossed the board planks and went down the path leading to where the cold, clear water flowed from the side of the riverbank, cascading down to the river. They soon learned a pail full of water was not an easy thing to handle as they scrambled back up the incline. Both boys together managed to get it back on the road where they set it down and rested.

"How we gonna do it?"

"You take it first since it was your idea. Then, I'll carry it a ways," said Ralph.

Don picked up the pail, holding his left arm out for balance. The pail banged against his legs, sloshing out some of the water.

"You're spilling it," observed Rate.

"I know. Like to see you do any better."

"Guess probably I could at that."

"Here. You take it then."

Ralph took the pail, but after a few steps, he banged it against his leg and sloshed water on his pants.

"You sloshed it too," pointed out Curly. Rate set the pail down.

"Guess we'd better try carrying it together. Maybe that will work better."

Don took one side and Rate the other. Both lifted together on the bail, but the pail seemed to bang around worse than ever.

"This ain't no better, Rate. What we gonna do?"

"It was your idea. You figger it out."

Rate sat down on the roadside and looked at his friend. Don, who was usually so self-assured, looked completely baffled.

"I've got it," cried Rate. "We weren't in step. Let's try it again. We'll both start off with our right foot and then see."

They took up their positions, and sure enough, keeping in step helped. Slowly and surely, they made their way back to the schoolhouse. If the pail wasn't quite as full as usual, no one said anything. Miss Peabody smiled to herself when the boys slid into their seats. She had watched their progress out of the window and knew they had nearly bitten off more than they could chew. She was almost certain neither of them would ask for that task again, and she was right, they never did.

*****

Miney had driven to town by herself to get groceries since Millie needed to get some feed ground for the hogs.

There seemed to be an unusual amount of activity at the mill when Millie and Rate drove up. Several men were standing in a group, talking excitedly about something. Millie threw off his bags onto the loading platform and then joined the group to see what was going on.

Mr. Cooley, the owner, was in the center.

"Just don't know why such a thing had to happen."

"What's going on?" asked Millie.

"We've just had us a drowning," said Cooley.

"A drowning? Who?"

"Little Harry Newington, Amza's boy."

"How in tarnation did something like that happen?"

"Seems he and his brother had been down there in the basement. The older boy wanted to come ask his pa something, so he cautioned the little fellow to stay away from where the boards cover the flume. When he went back down, he couldn't find Harry, so he gave a yell, and we all came runnin'. One of the boards looked askew, so we took up the others and used a rake to search. Sure enough, at the other end, against the grating, was his body. You know, it didn't take much of a hole for a five-year-old lad to slip through. That water in the flume isn't all that deep, but it is so swift, the tyke didn't have no chance at'all."

"Just never know how long a person has, do you? Kids always have to try just what they've been told not to do," said Millie.

"The brother took it pretty hard. Think he was a feared Amza was going to blame him. Right then, Amza was too broken up to put blame on anyone. 'Sides, it ain't like the boy did it on purpose."

"What in hell were they down there for?" asked someone.

"Don't rightly know. No one seen 'em go."

Rate had been standing to one side and had heard the conversation. My gosh, first Ed and now some little boy—both dead because of an accident. He had always known the water flowed fast through the mill to turn the two huge waterwheels set horizontally under the building. In fact, Pa had cautioned him to stay away from the bank that led to the millrace because when the doors were open, the water flowed through with enough force that Pa had explained a person would have been sucked under and held against the grating, which kept out debris, even if that person could swim. Rate had been given to understand that the millrace deserved a lot of respect. Made him wonder why Mr. Newington hadn't impressed this on his boys. Perhaps he had tried, but perhaps he was not as severe in his punishment as Pa, so his boys felt they didn't have to mind. Maybe Pa was so blamed strict for his own good.

*****

Millie decided it was high time the lambs were sold. He and Jim Keenan drove them onto the barn floor, and from there, they loaded them onto the wagon, which was equipped with a high rack so even the most agile or frightened lamb could not jump over it. They had already made one trip to St. Johns, where the largest stockyards were located, and were now about to leave with the second load.

Millie stepped into the dining room and spied Ralph sitting cross-legged on the floor, playing with a small cast-iron fire engine, pulled by coal-black horses, which was one of his favorite toys.

"Rate, Jim and I are leaving with another load of lambs. We've got yours this time. How much will you take for him?"

Rate pondered the question, then piped up, "I'll take a dollar for him."

"Boy, you've made yourself a sale."

Millie reached into his pocket, took out a silver dollar, and rolled it across the floor to his son. Without another word, he turned and left.

A whole dollar! He had almost been afraid to ask Pa for that much money, but Pa hadn't even tried to Jew him down—just forked over the dollar, a nice shiny one too. Boy, a dollar to do with just as he pleased. He had sure earned it feeding those lambs for all those weeks. Not that he had minded most of the time, but there had been a few days when he would have liked to play hockey and forgot about bottles for seven lambs.

Rate's feeling of euphoria continued until the day when Millie received the check in payment for the lambs. Ralph noticed the satisfied look on his father's face and heard him tell Miney, "We got a good price for the lambs. Best we've had for quite a spell."

Rate asked his father how much they had received, and Millie told him the amount of the check. Rate still did not have the information he was fishing for; he wanted to know how much each lamb brought. Well, he knew how many lambs they had; however, he hadn't learned that much about ciphering. When Ma wasn't busy, he would ask her, being certain she would figure it out for him.

Miney finished the dinner dishes, removed her apron, and sat down with some crocheting; Millie and Jim had gone back outside to return to the work they had interrupted for the noon meal.

Rate took this opportunity to ask Miney the all-important question. He told her how many lambs they had sold, what Pa got for them, and then asked the question.

"Ma, how much money was that for each lamb?"

"Well, Ralph, I'd have to figure it out. Now, let's see. Unless I made a mistake, it was just a few cents over three dollars apiece."

"Three dollars! Are you sure?"

Mentally, she ran over the figures again and said, "Yes, that's right. Three dollars and about twenty cents, I didn't figure it exactly."

Three dollars a head, and he'd sold his lamb to Pa for one measly dollar. Pa had made two dollars on his lamb. Ralph knew there would be no use complaining to his father that it was unfair because Millie had asked him what he wanted for the lamb, and he had set his own price. Bet he'd never sell anything again without knowing the fair market value. A dollar had seemed like a good price, only compared to three, it was merely a drop in the bucket.

*****

As so often happened, Vere Brown had sure riled Miss Peabody this morning. Vere, who was a grade behind Rate, often seemed to vex his teacher. For one thing, Vere did not take his schoolwork seriously, so he seldom had his assignments done at class recitation time. This morning had been worse than usual.

Vere had not had his work done for his arithmetic class, then he had been disruptive at his seat; Miss Peabody had stood him in the corner, so close his nose was almost touching the wall, but he kept turning around, when she wasn't looking, causing the kids to laugh because he was making faces. Finally, in desperation, she had jerked him out of the corner and shoved him underneath her desk. The teacher's desk was crudely built of heavy boards with drawers on each side and a kneehole in the middle. It was situated so there was no way Vere could peek out at any classmates.

Just before dinner, Miss Peabody gave Vere permission to return to his seat.

He grinned a little sheepishly and amazingly went right to work.

It was noon, time for dinner. Books were put away, dinner pails brought from a shelf in the respective cloakrooms, each student bowed his head while the teacher said grace, and then the hungry children looked to see what their mother had packed for the day. Rate always had meat or egg sandwiches although a lot of students had only jelly—slightly soaked into the bread—for sandwiches.

"Land's sakes," exclaimed Miss Peabody.

The talking stopped, and each student looked her way wondering what was amiss. She held up an empty dinner pail. No one even snickered, but all eyes turned to Vere, who sat in his seat as unconcerned as could be, wolfing down a jelly sandwich.

"Vere Brown," came the stern voice. "Come here."

Smiling somewhat abashedly, Vere slid out of his seat and slowly approached the teacher's desk. Thereupon, he hung his head and looked at the scuffed toes of his shoes, not knowing if he dare grin or not.

"Vere, what happened to my dinner?"

The boy shifted from one foot to another and mumbled a reply.

"Speak up. I couldn't understand you."

"I-I…aw…Miss Peabody, I et it."

"Didn't you know that was wrong?"

"Reckon so, but I din't have no breakfast, an' I wuz hongry. I'm sorry. Is ya gonna lick me?"

"Vere, Vere. I don't honestly know what I'm going to do with you. You go back and finish your own dinner."

"Already did. Only had one sannich," he explained.

Goodness, a growing boy needed more than that to eat; little wonder that he had not been able to resist the temptation of her dinner. Well, she supposed she'd have to keep him after school and make him wash the blackboards or perhaps bring in kindling. It was cold enough to have a small fire most of the day now, so each night, wood had to be brought from the woodshed and piled by the stove for use the next day. She couldn't ignore the fact that the boy had taken something that did not belong to him, even if she did understand the reason.

*****

Miney was upset. She had just this day received some disturbing news in a letter from her sister Ettie. Miney had read and reread the middle portion.

I just learned that I am in the family way. Miney, whatever am I to do? Why, I'm almost forty years old, and I just know I'll die having this baby. Look how old Glen and Free are. I haven't been one bit well, and I've told George how terrible I feel. I know he just thinks I'm being silly—says there's no need for me to worry, plenty of women my age have babies. Men are just heartless and unfeeling. I was always so sick before the boys were born, and I just know this is going to be worse. Don't suppose it would be quite so bad if I wanted another child, but I don't. Never actually wanted the boys, only once they were here, I loved them. George simply does not understand how I feel. Guess if he'd had his way, we'd have had a dozen. At least some of the time he realizes that my health is delicate at best. I just told him that this is all his fault, and when

I'm dead and gone, he can just realize who it was who put me in my grave.

There was more, but Miney gave that a cursory glance and reread the middle again. Her heart went out to Ettie. Good heavens, imagine being forced to have a baby at forty. Miney had always been fond of George and thought he had been very understanding of some of Ettie's eccentricities; now, she felt angry with him. Goodness, how old did a man have to be before he no longer needed to satisfy his desires? She agreed with Ettie— it was all George's fault. If a man didn't always force his attentions on a woman, but she guessed that was asking for too much. She would write to Ettie tonight and see what she could do to put her sister in a better frame of mind. If Ettie was determined that having a child would kill her—it likely would. Miney decided to do what she could to improve her sister's outlook although it was going to be extremely difficult since Miney shared Ettie's beliefs as well as apprehensions.

That evening, after the children had gone to bed, she told Millie about Ettie's letter.

"Forty isn't all that old. If Ettie would only forget about her health, get interested in something for a change, she'd feel better."

"How do you know she would? You've never been forced to have a baby."

"Don't think she was forced either. Still, there's many a slip twixt the cup and the lip."

"It is all George's fault. Wonder if he will feel like a murderer when Ettie dies."

"You sound as though her death is inevitable. She isn't dead yet, so don't cross your bridges afore you get to them"

"I just know she has a woman's intuition. Men can't understand these things. I know Ettie has a premonition, and I'll warrant it is right."

"Humph," grunted Millie.

As far as he was concerned, Ettie was a little willy-nilly and a chronic complainer. She had complained so much about Doc that he'd given up medicine and become a lawyer. Millie felt that Ettie would be glad to die just to prove to the world that what she said was right. He bet poor Doc's life would be nothing but pure, unadulterated hell until that baby was born.

He was reminded of how Miney had treated him when she was carrying Ralph, always telling him it was his fault. If he knew Ettie, she'd be ten times worse than Miney ever was. Sometimes, he wondered if all women resented the intimate relations between a husband and wife.

Ma had never complained about having children—only about losing them after they got here. She had finally convinced Pa it was likely his sinful ways, and that was probably the biggest reason Pa had got religion. Hadn't made any difference, Millie thought, because even though Pa had been going to church ever Sunday in atonement, they had lost little Emma anyway. He guessed women just weren't happy if they didn't have a man to blame for something.

*****

It was Sunday morning, and while Ralph had been up to do his chores, he had gone to change his clothes for church.

"Ralph," called Mina at the stairway door leading upstairs to the children's rooms. "Ralph, you be sure and bring your dirty clothes down for the wash tomorrow. And don't forget to change your suit of underwear."

"But, Ma, I changed it last week."

"You didn't either. It was your father's suit I had in the wash last week. Didn't you put on your clean one this morning?"

"No. Shall I change now? I'm almost dressed," he added plaintively.

"Hurry and change. I'll not have you going to church dirty."

It never occurred to Miney that there would be a time when folks would change their winter underwear any more often than every other week. Those heavy, woolen flannel, long-legged underwear suits were dreadful to wash and dry, so she had Millie and Ralph change on alternate weeks. Woman's suits were not quite as bulky, so hers and Blanche's were not nearly the trouble. Some womenfolk said they only washed their menfolk's suits once a month, but Miney figured they would be rather smelly in that length of time. Two weeks' wear, and then a good scrubbing was much better. Of course, Ralph, like any growing boy, had to be reminded, or he would never think to change his clothes less'n maybe they got so's they would stand alone.

Rate hastily doffed his outer pants to strip off his dirty underwear, first having the clean suit ready to don as quickly as possible. Sure was cold upstairs although winter hadn't yet set in fiercely enough for him to dress downstairs by the fire. When he was just a child, he had always grabbed his clothes and hightailed it down the stairs to the welcome warmth of the dining room stove. Now that he was bigger, he stuck it out except in the very coldest weather of December and January. He was sure this had not been his week to change, but from past experience, he knew it was useless to argue with his mother.

He finished dressing, put on his long black woolen socks, and stuck his feet into icy-cold shoes. Oh, well, he would warm his feet on the fender of the stove when he got downstairs.

He picked up his underwear and wrinkled up his nose as he smelled it. The pungent odor of turpentine and goose grease assailed his nostrils. Guess he had worn it longer than he supposed since it was a week ago yesterday that Ma had started doctoring him for a cold on his chest. She had made a concoction of goose grease laced with turpentine to rub on his chest. She had also given him some of the catnip tea that she steeped every fall for just such emergencies. He liked the heavy onion syrup she had made from boiling onions in a small amount of water, then sweetening it with sugar until it made a heavy syrup much thicker than the maple syrup they used on pancakes. He had even carried a small bottle to school in case he got a fit of coughing there.

Come to think of it, half the kids in school smelled of turpentine since this was the time-honored remedy of most parents. At least he had never had to take chicken manure like Pa. With a mother like Grandmother Setterington, there would have been no talking her out of it either.

Thinking of his grandmother brought another thing to mind. He had heard his grandfather and Pa talking one day, and Grandfather had said something about moving to another town. Now, that really would make a change in their lives not to have Grandmother and Grandfather around. Bet Ma would like it a heap better without her bossy mother-in-law looking down her nose at everything Ma did and always telling Ma how she should do things. Pa just never seemed to mind. Guess he'd grown so used to being bossed by his parents as a little shaver, it had just been a habit to let them continue to boss him around. Ma would have liked to rebel, for it sure went against her grain to knuckle under all the time.

If they left Elsie, he wondered what Blanche would do. Blanche was perfectly capable of driving back and forth to school, only sometimes Ma sure did want her pampered. Sometimes, he wasn't sure Blanche liked staying with her grandparents since she often was headstrong, and she never quite gave in to her grandmother's whims—only on the surface while the inner girl seethed.

Mina was darning a pair of Ralph's socks while Blanche sat at the table putting the hem in the housedress they had just finished making for her.

"Ma, why don't Grandmother and Grandfather like Aunt Grace?"

"Lawsy, Blanche, who says they dislike her?"

"Well, for one thing, the girls at school talk. Then Grandmother is always finding fault with Aunt Grace. 'I'll never understand what Johnny saw in her. Grace just always overdresses. She just never knows how to dress suitably. If only she would attend church. Blood will tell,'" she imitated. "Grandmother always talks like that. What does she mean 'blood will tell'?"

"I presume she means that Grace is adopted, so she really isn't a Cobb. Of course, no one knows who her natural parents were."

"Uncle John hasn't accomplished much, if you ask me, so why does she act like Aunt Grace is so much worse?"

"Well, her son just has to be better than someone else. I guess your grandmother thinks he married beneath him. Still, I'm of a mind that John was no bargain. Leastwise he has never been a steady worker like your father. Then, too, Grace sometimes argues with your grandmother, and you know for a fact Mother Setterington cannot tolerate anyone disagreeing with her."

"That's true enough. If I voice an opinion, it is always wrong according to her. You know how Grandmother is always asking what we want for Christmas. Well, you should have seen the list Uncle John gave her. She grumbled to Grandfather something awful, but she's already started buying the things he wanted. Guess it was practical since most of it was warm clothes for the kids. If she gets it all, Aunt Grace and Uncle John won't have to buy the kids any winter clothes. Of course, I suppose if we gave her a list, she'd buy what we want too."

"I presume she would, but that makes Christmas so commercial somehow. The giving of gifts is all right, only we must not forget that we celebrate Christmas because that was when Christ was born. That is the important thing. I don't think there have to be a lot of gifts, or expensive ones either, and they should come as a surprise to the one who receives them."

"I think so too. Only it just made me wonder why Grandmother is so generous when she always finds so much fault."

"Blanche, your grandmother has always been a mystery to me. I think she thrives on finding fault with others. You'll notice Ruby never comes in for her share though. Mother never says one word against Mac, and he hasn't always been the best provider. Of course, Mother always paid for a hired girl so Ruby wouldn't have to do the heavy work."

"Seems as though Grandmother wants to run everyone's life. I'll never let her run mine, you can count on that."

Mina glanced up at her daughter and noticed the set line to her mouth. The girl was right, thought Mina. I think maybe

Mother has met her match here. Blanche is too much like Mother to be intimidated by her. Don't know as I like her being quite so strong-willed and spunky, but I do want her to lead her own life without interference from her grandmother. I expect there will be more than one clash of wills before Blanche is grown.

Christmas that year was especially nice. Rate got the usual amount of clothes—each year like clockwork, he had a pair of double knit gloves from Aunt Lorin—a book or two, but the present that left him wide- eyed and almost tongue-tied was the beautiful air rifle and huge box of BBs from Grandmother and Grandfather. He had been rather enviously eyeing Blanche's *The Adventures of a Brownie*, which had come from Aunt Ruby since the title certainly sounded enticing to Ralph; however, in all fairness, he had to admit he could not read that well yet. This inability had in no way kept him from wishing. Then had come the gun. My oh my, what a beautiful sight it was. Maybe Grandmother and Grandfather did like him as much as they did Blanche; well, anyway, they had given him a really nice present.

Ralph was soon to learn that his mother did not approve of the gun for a present—said he was still too young. He'd heard her and Pa discussing the matter. Well, maybe discussing wasn't quite the word since Ma had been doing all the talking, and Pa was just keeping still like usual.

"Millie, Ralph is too young to have a gun even if it isn't a real one. It still shoots those little pellets, and I don't think it is a safe thing for him to have. It's just like your mother to give him something like that without asking our opinion. Supposing he gets hurt or shoots one of the neighbor children?"

"Now, Miney, first of all, the lad's got sense. He's going to be careful, and those popguns aren't much anyway. Personally, I thought it a mighty fine gift. I'll be sure he knows how to use it safely, so I don't want to hear any more about it."

Miney knew from the tone as much as the words that it would be futile to argue further. "I just hope you're right," she muttered, half to herself.

Ralph was always one for getting into trouble, and giving him an air gun was just asking for some disaster to happen. She had told him that he could not use the gun when any of his friends were over. At least that would take care of the risk of having him accidentally shoot someone. True, a BB gun couldn't kill a person, but it could most assuredly put out an eye.

Perhaps Millie was right. Perhaps she was overprotective of Ralph and didn't want him to live the life of a boy. If only he had been a girl—no use pursuing that line of thought because she couldn't change the situation. Still, she knew more about what to do with girls, and a lively normal boy like her son was rather bewildering at times.

If only he wasn't always getting into mischief or trouble of some sort. But she guessed Millie liked him that way. Leastways, there were many things he encouraged; just like them always scuffling, and that always set Bruno barking until finally he'd join in the fracas to take Ralph's part. Sometimes, she thought it was a wonder that some furniture hadn't been broken during one of the wrestling sessions. Ralph always got the worst of it, but that still didn't stop him from starting it. Guess he was always in hopes that with the element of surprise on his side, he would be able to best his father sometime.

Raising children did take a lot of doing especially when one was a boy. Ma had been lucky to have all girls, and yet she recalled that her mother had often said she would have liked a son. Guess maybe Ma had wished she had known Pa's boys when they were small. Maybe that was so there would have been some family ties because after their father died, they hadn't seen fit to pay hardly any attention to their stepmother. 'Course, to be truthful, they hadn't seen much of Pa after they had married and had moved away.

Jim had been the restless one, always on the move, always looking for a better place. He had made those trips to Oregon by wagon train in the hopes of becoming rich, only each time he came back, he had been broke. Pa had always said Jim was a good worker for a year or two, and then his itchy foot began to bother, and off he would go. None of Pa's boys had been the homebody Pa was.

Miney missed her parents. Pa had been an interesting storyteller, and Ma had always been easy to talk to. If she complained to Ma about Ralph's antics, Ma always had some words of wisdom to make her feel better. 'Course, Ma had always thought a lot of Ralph. Perhaps it was because he was the youngest grandchild. She had plenty of grandsons: Lorin's Georgie, Mary's Frank, and Ettie's Glen and Free. Anyway, Ma had never shown partiality between Ralph and Blanche. Miney knew that she herself often favored Blanche, and try as she might, she couldn't help loving Blanche the most. Not that she didn't love Ralph—he was such a good-looking lad and usually very good-natured—it was just that he did manage to try her patience. Well, she would just have to keep asking the good Lord to help her out, for He knew she certainly couldn't do this job of raising children alone.

Ralph and Bruno were out in the yard romping together. A few days ago, Millie had brought Rate a dog harness, and Ralph had been trying to teach Bruno to haul the sled. At first, the dog had objected to all those straps of leather and had tried to bite and tug to get them off. Ralph had patiently worked with the young dog who now tolerated the harness. However, Rate had not tried to hitch him up as yet. At least Bruno would follow Rate anywhere without getting upset with all that leather hanging on his body. Ralph had made up his mind that today was to be the big day. Much to his surprise, the dog did not object. He simply pulled the sled wherever Rate called him.

That night, after supper, Ralph spoke to his mother.

"Ma, do you need some apples brought home from Clark's?"

This year, Millie had decided it was too much work to pit apples, so they had stored some of the crop in the Clarks' basement. Millie had been bringing them home a crate at a time.

"Why, yes, I could use some more. Millie, are there any apples left at Ed's?"

"Three or four crates, if I recollect right."

"Why are you so anxious to get apples? Last time, when you had to get some on your sled, you did nothing but complain."

Miney eyed her son suspiciously.

"I just thought I'd offer."

"You didn't answer my question."

"All right. It's 'cause I've taught Bruno to pull the sled. I figured I'd have him help me."

"So that's it. In other words, you won't have to do the work, Bruno will."

"Something like that," he admitted, giving her a smile.

"Land's sakes, do you think that dog is strong enough to pull that much weight?"

"He can pull me all right."

"I suppose you can try it," said Miney.

The next night after school, Ralph hitched his dog to the sled and made the trip to the Clarks' on the Ridge. Ed helped him bring up a crate of apples from the basement to place on the sled. At first, strain as he might, Bruno could not get the sled to move. Ralph got behind it and gave a shove. There it went! However, since the drive was slightly uphill, Ralph continued to push until they were in the road and headed for home. Bruno pulled with a will, seemingly enjoying his job. Ralph's murmurs of "Good boy, Bruno." "Attaboy." "You can do it." only served to urge the dog to a steady, rapid walk. This certainly was better than having to pull the sled himself, thought Ralph. Good ole Bruno. He sure was a good dog and a mighty smart one too.

*****

Millie had come home through the mire that only slightly resembled a road. The rig and horses were both caked with half-dried clumps of mud. He was glad he had braided the horses' tails so they had not dragged in the slime. As it was, he knew he'd have to soak and wash Major's feet. Major was half Clydesdale, and that profuse amount of hair growing around each hoof had to be cleaned and soaked free of the icy mud particles if his feet were to be kept in good condition. It would have been much easier if the hair could have been trimmed off, only Millie knew that if this was done, a Clydesdale usually got scabies. Why those little parasites felt they had to pick on the poor Clydesdale, Millie never knew, but he and others had learned the hard way that the good Lord had given the horse all that hair for a reason.

Millie had a bit of news for Miney. The ice had gone out of the river and had jammed up against the new bridge in such a wild assortment of chunks, there had been some concern for the bridge itself. Men had even contemplated using dynamite to break up the mountain of ice lodged against the lower part of the bridge. However, there were those against this idea, and while they were arguing the pros and cons of the advisability of blasting the ice, nature had taken care of the situation. Now, they were arguing as to whether the bridge had been built too close to the water. There were those in favor of going to the expense of raising the bridge two feet, and there were those opposed. Millie felt that raising it would be a bunch of nonsense. It had withstood this ice jam, and like as not, there wouldn't be another one for years. The old wooden bridge had been nearer the water, and the ice had never destroyed it. No use borrowing trouble, and Millie felt trying to raise a bridge of that size was certainly asking for trouble.

It was true. Grandmother and Grandfather were moving the first of April. Rate wasn't just sure why as yet, and he didn't rightly care because he thought it was funny that Blanche no longer would have a place to stay. Ma had asked Blanche if she wanted to stay with Aunt Lorin, but Blanche didn't seem to cotton to the idea. She had said that it was a shame Aunt Mary and Uncle Jap had moved 'cause she would sure liked to have stayed with Aunt Mary, who was the grandest person and was her most favorite aunt.

A number of years ago, Mary and Jasper Sickles had moved north from Elsie into timber country where Jap had started a sawmill. Now, there was a little community there, and it was called Sickles after the original settler. They had moved from there to Chicago. Ralph remembered visiting them once, and it had been fun. Of course, they didn't have anyone for him to play with since Frank was lots older. Lelah was Blanche's age, so that was one more reason Blanche liked being with them. 'Course Aunt Mary reminded both of them of Grandma—at least more so than anyone else.

The weeks passed quickly, and Lovina and Horatio moved to South Lyon, where Horatio started a private bank. He had $16,000 in cash of his own money, and while it was perhaps not a spectacular amount, it was sufficient capital for the times. He still had numerous land holdings throughout Clinton, Gratiot, and Shiawassee counties, so if the occasion demanded, he could have raised at least twice that amount. However, he was getting a good return for his money invested, so he would let the situation remain as it was for the time being.

Ralph learned that Uncle Mac and Aunt Ruby had moved from Big Rapids to be with Grandfather in South Lyon. Since Uncle Mac was a bookkeeper, he presumed this was the reason Grandfather had given Uncle Mac the job.

However, he had heard his parents talking, and Pa had said, "Pa just took Mac into the business so Ma could have Ruby near her. Well, if Mac is ever to amount to a picayune, it will have to be because he rode there on Pa's coattails."

Rate wasn't quite sure what his father meant. Ma had said something about Ruby being so spoiled, and the way everyone doted on her now that Lois had been born was a sight for sore eyes. Personally, Ralph didn't think much of Lois. 'Course she was so tiny she couldn't even sit up by herself yet. Maybe if she'd been a boy, he would have been more interested.

After much haggling and discussing, it was agreed that Blanche could finish out the school year by driving back and forth to Elsie. Millie still had that dependable old mare, Topsy, or Old Mikey, and Blanche could stable either one in Grandfather's barn since he had not yet sold his house.

Miney had mixed emotions about it. She most assuredly wanted her daughter home with her, only she didn't take a notion to Blanche's having to drive. She was still more upset when Millie decided that since Blanche had to drive to Elsie five days a week, she might as well take their milk to the cheese factory there. He had been taking it himself each day to Knight's cheese factory over west, only there were rumors they were going to close, so now he figured this would save him the trouble, and it might not be a bad idea to get started somewhere else. While Blanche might not have been too thrilled with this idea, she also knew better than to voice any sort of dissension.

A few days before she was to start driving, Ed Clark came over to talk with her. Ed owned the farm west on the Ridge Road just past Sherman's woods, so part of his land bordered the back of Millie's eighty.

Ed had a proposition to make for Blanche.

"Blanche, since you'll be haulin' milk to the cheese factory fer yore pa, how 'ud you like to pick up a can fer me?"

"Well, I don't know—"

"I'll pay you say fifty cents a week. How 'ud thet be? Won't take much extree work, and you kin have some spendin' money. Be it agreed?"

"All right. I'll do it," answered Blanche.

The chance to earn money was a great incentive. Trouble was, she didn't know that Ed would never pay her a single, solitary cent, and her folks wouldn't let her ask him for what he owed, saying he was a good neighbor in other ways.

Blanche hated hauling milk. The cheese factory was on the east side of town, over a block off the main street, and had an odor all its own. Sometimes, she had to wait in line because there were several farmers ahead of her, and it nearly made her late for school.

There was a place where the milk was dumped, then she had to drive on a little farther and collect the hot whey, which came out of a canvas tube. Old Sam Packingham was the one who pumped the wooden handle to force the whey up into the tube, which he also controlled. The factory had tried once to let the farmers pump their own whey, but this had not worked out well at all. It seemed that some folks who only sold a very small amount of milk—and therefore had contributed an equally small amount of whey to the total amount—helped themselves overgenerously; thus, they ran out of whey before everyone had collected his allotment. This was why Sam tried to portion it out so everyone got some. It didn't always work out this way, and on occasion, they had pumped out the entire day's allotment before the last patrons came to collect.

Sam had lost a leg in the Civil War. He stumped around on his peg leg and, to Blanche, always seemed in a grouchy mood. More often than not, he missed with the first or last bits of whey, so it ran all over the floor of the springboard wagon. My, it did stink, and the flies sure did swarm.

Both Millie and Ed had pigs, and they wanted the whey to feed to them; thus, there was no way Blanche could be excused from getting their allotment of whey.

Blanche had to hurry back to Grandfather's house, put the horse in the stable, and then dash the two blocks to school. Of course, she still cut through by Grandma Smith's house, which did make it some shorter. Anyway, she always felt hot and messy when she arrived. Town girls never had to work like this—they maybe made their own bed or did the breakfast dishes, which wasn't very time-consuming. Guess maybe underneath she felt that this really was man's work; however, Pa wasn't one to argue with, especially when it concerned work.

Then, at night, after the whey was fed to the hogs, she or Ma or both worked at scrubbing out the stale, stinking whey, which clung tenaciously to the sides of the milk can. Then, the can had to be scalded with boiling hot water so it wouldn't turn tomorrow's milk sour. These thirty-gallon cans were large and cumbersome and difficult for the two women to handle. When full of milk, it took a good man like Millie to toss one easily onto the wagon.

At least old Topsy was an easy horse to drive and nothing seemed to frighten her; she just plodded along at her set gait. Even if Blanche was to touch her lightly with the whip, it only speeded her up for a few steps, and then she dropped right back to her regular gait, which was no more than a fast walk.

Half the time, before she could come home, Blanche had to stop at the general store to buy something for Ma. Actually, she felt her mother rather liked having her drive to school so she could get something from town every day. Much of it could have been bought when Ma shopped on Saturday, but for some reason, Ma always was forgetting something. Either that or Ma preferred to spend her grocery money a few cents at a time. Ma sure did like to pinch a penny. Bet when she grew up, she would be better than her mother at planning her shopping trips.

CHAPTER 7

April is traditionally the season of warm spring rains to awake the dormant vegetation, the time of rebirth. This year was no exception. The expression "April showers bring May flowers" had certainly held true this year because the mayflowers had already carpeted the woodlots with their delicate, pale pink because the last few days had been unseasonably warm. The woodlots were also full of puddles and marshy spots, and even the roadsides were much wetter than usual. The Ridge, because of its sandy composition, was normally well dried off by this time of year; however, such was not the case this year.

Blanche hated the wet spring even if it was a warm one. Some days she drove the wagon, but after being thoroughly wetted in a shower on the way to school, she had used the buggy even if it was more difficult to fit the milk cans on the back. She often wondered why the rain usually came in the afternoon when she was going home since most of the time, any wind also came from the southwest, driving the rain into the buggy, thoroughly soaking her. Now, in the morning, the wind would have been to her back, and she'd have had the protection of the buggy and side curtains.

Today was no exception. Blanche managed to get Old Mikey hitched to the buggy before the first splatters of rain began. There were large pelting drops, which came violently at first, lessened, then came violently again, and then quit altogether. Just maybe she could get home before the storm really broke. Huge black clouds were swirling in from the southwest, and Blanche watched them anxiously as she urged Old Mikey to a fast trot. At least his speed was greater than Topsy's.

She crossed the river and turned north by the cemetery before the rain commenced again. This time, the drops were small and wind-driven, and with each step that Old Mikey took, it seemed the storm increased in intensity. When Blanche turned west once more, the rain blew in sheets as the clouds dumped their cargo, the road became obliterated, and Blanche was immediately drenched.

She began to cry, her tears mingling with the rainwater running down her face. It was difficult to keep her eyes open; she wanted only to close them against the driving rain.

"Oh, Mikey, Mikey. What are we to do? I can't see the road, and I'm near soaked to the skin."

The old black horse, wise in so many ways, felt the lines slacken. In a moment, he had turned the buggy around in the road; he hung his head and hunched his rump to the lashing rain.

Blanche sighed with relief as now the top and sides of the buggy were bearing the brunt of the storm. No longer was the rain stinging her face; her clothes might be sodden and stuck to her in their wetness, but she was more comfortable.

"Good Old Mikey. You know more than I do. This is much better," she murmured.

When the storm had pretty much abated, Mikey lifted his head, glanced back at Blanche, nickered softly, then turned back to head for home where they found Millie anxiously awaiting his daughter whom he sent directly to the house to get out of her wet clothes while he took care of the horse.

Blanche let it be known that Old Mikey had had more good sense than she had. She ended by saying, "But, Pa, I remembered what you always said about not stopping under a tree. There were a couple of big ones, and they are all leaved out, but I minded what you said."

"Good for you, Blanche. Lightning does strike a tree now and again, so they just aren't safe."

"It was an awful temptation all the same. Old Mikey sure was a blessing. Guess I did learn something today."

Miney was busy rearranging Blanche's dress and coat where they hung near the stove to dry. She was worried for fear Blanche would take a cold, but her fears were unfounded; being strong and healthy, Blanche suffered no ill effects from her drenching.

The latter part of March, Clayt Sherman had moved off the farm. Swarthout, the tenant who had moved there the following week, had several children. It hadn't taken Rate long to become friends with Rollie, who was in his grade at school. Frankie was lots older, so he didn't always want Rollie and Rate tagging him around. There were some girls, but Ralph figured girls were only made to tease, and there were times when Rollie's sisters felt like skinning both boys alive if they could only have caught them. If Rollie had been somewhat of a tease before, he only became worse with Ralph around to help him think of ideas.

It had been one of those days when whatever Rate could think of to do didn't exactly appeal to him. It was still wet from April rains, and the day was more than a bit on the cold side, with a hint of still more rain in the angry black clouds swirling overhead, so playing baseball didn't suit his fancy either. He had thrown a few stones with his slingshot, but quickly became bored. Bruno followed his master faithfully, obviously puzzled by his random wanderings. They went into the toolshed where Ralph poked around in the litter of odds and ends.

"Jeepers, Bruno. Look what I found. This stuff in this old jar is gunpowder sure as shootin'. Pa don't need it no more. He don't hunt much, and he's been buyin' his shells at Downey's. Bet we'd get a bang out of this just like a big firecracker. C'mon, Bruno. Let's go see."

Bruno sat on his haunches, tilting his head from side to side, ears perked forward, watching Rate's every move. Now, he bounded after the boy, not understanding, but ready to follow wherever the boy might lead. He watched as the boy carried out back of the granary the two-quart jar that was nearly full of black gunpowder.

141

Rate plunked the can on the ground, rummaged around to find a length of board that he laid on the ground; next he poured the gunpowder in a small thin line from one end of the board to the other where he dumped the excess into a small pile.

"Now, Bruno, you stay back over here whilst I light this."

The dog obediently sat where Rate pointed. The lad fished around in his pockets and came up with two matches. He struck a match and held it to the dribbled-out fuse. It burned a few inches, then went out as the powder became too thin to carry it further. Ralph sighed in disgust, lighted the second match, and held it to the heavier line, which was much nearer the pile. *Whoosh!* Before he had more than dropped the match, the whole pile went up in one big puff of fire and smoke. Rate grabbed his face with his hands. Golly, but he had never expected results like this. He guessed he was all right. He didn't seem to be burned. Bruno whined and carried on until Rate absently patted his head.

"It's all right, Bruno. Don't guess I'm hurt any, but it seems like I can smell singed hair. Guess I'll go take a look-see."

While the acrid smell of burned gunpowder clung to the air, there was also the unmistakable odor of scorched hair. Rate entered the house rather cautiously having no desire to meet his mother until he had assessed his own damage.

"Ralph?" came the query. "That you? What do you want?"

"Nothin', Ma. I just got tired of being outside."

He headed for the stairway, but his mother came from the kitchen before he had more than put his hand on the doorknob.

"Ralph, are you hiding something?"

"No, Ma. I was just goin' upstairs."

"With those dirty shoes? Not much you aren't. Come back here and clean them off on the porch. When will you ever learn?"

Heaving a resigned sigh, Rate turned around.

"Goodness! Whatever have you been into now? Your face is blackened, and, and—why, you have no eyebrows, and even your hair is singed. Ralph Setterington, whatever have you been doing?" she demanded, her tone unmistakably stern.

"Nothin' much."

"Do you call getting your eyebrows singed off nothing? Your hair is singed where it sticks out from under your stocking cap. Did it scorch the cap?"

"Naw. Golly, Ma, I didn't do it on purpose. I just found this can of old gunpowder, and I took it out and set fire to it. I thought it would explode like a firecracker, but it jest burnt, and I didn't even have no time to get away it went so fast. Honest, I didn't intend to get singed."

"I suppose not," she conceded. "Lucky you were that it wasn't worse. Clean your shoes, and then wash your face and hands. I'll have your father speak to you tonight."

"Yessum."

Land's sakes, would she ever live to see that boy grown to manhood— that is if he didn't kill himself before that time. If it wasn't one thing, it was another. She'd long ago lost track of how many nails he'd stepped on during the summer months when he went barefoot, how many skinned fingers, knees, and oh, just about everything. My, he would certainly look a sight to take to church tomorrow, only there wasn't much she could do about it.

True to her word, Miney related the incident to Millie when he came in to supper. In his usual manner, Millie listened to his wife, yet said not a word, his face completely expressionless.

Blanche hissed at Ralph, "You're in for it now. Pa looks sort of mad."

"Does not. He's just thinkin'."

"Bet you get walloped."

"Bet I don't," Ralph said much more bravely than he felt.

"Boy, is what your ma says true?"

Rate swallowed hard. "That's right, Pa. That gunpowder went up faster'n you could say *scat*."

"Come here." Rate moved toward his father. "Stand here where I can see you. You don't appear hurt none, but I guess you don't have much of any eyebrows or eyelashes left." He touched Rate's hair. "Looks like you got rid of a little here too."

Rate watched his father warily. Pa was so blamed hard to figure out. He couldn't tell whether his father was angry or not.

"Did you learn anything?"

"Sure did. I learned that gunpowder burns awful fast, and it ain't nothin' to be foolin' around with."

"See that you don't forget that."

With that statement, Ralph knew he was dismissed. He flashed Blanche a triumphant look as he moved away. Later that evening, he spoke smugly, "Told you so."

"You're just lucky. You deserved a lickin'. Ma thinks so too. Bet she wishes she'd a done it herself 'stead of leavin' it up to Pa. Why can't you ever stay out of trouble? Boys!"

Rate laughed at his sister. He liked her well enough, and she was a lot of fun to tease. She got awful mad at him sometimes, but sometimes she was nice to him; and if she bought candy, she often saved a stick for him. If one had to have a sister, he guessed he would rather have her than any other girl he knew.

"Miney," called Millie from the wagon seat, "come look."

"What is it, Millie? Goodness, what have you got there?"

"Maple trees." And true enough, the wagon box was piled high with saplings.

"Whatever are you going to do with them?"

"Plant them. What else?"

"I know. But where?"

"I don't know for certain. Some in the yard and some along the road. Wouldn't some nice maples look good along the road?"

"I…well, I guess so. Guess I'd never given it much thought."

"Jim and I will get them planted soon's we eat dinner."

Later on, there were four new maples in the front of the house, maples between the south and north driveway, maples along the road north of the driveway, and maples along the road south of the front yard.

Rate had watched with interest. Upon completion, Millie had explained to his son that if these new trees were to live, they must be watered every day unless it rained. That was to be Ralph's job.

He could use Major on the stoneboat and fill a thirty-gallon milk can with water and give each tree a good pailful of water. At the telling, it hadn't sounded so bad, but in actual practice, Rate found it was not the most desirable of jobs. The worst job was filling the blamed milk can in the first place. Seemed like it was going to be a long summer.

*****

Ralph, Burl, and Don were finished with their work. Instead of rereading their reading assignment as they should have done, they started whispering. Don and Rate shared a double desk while Burl sat across the aisle; their desks were located near the back of the room on the north side in the first row by the stove. The small children sat here since it was warmer in the winter; the larger boys sat on the south side near the windows, which was more than a little chilly on a cold, windy winter's day, no matter if the stove was kept red hot.

However, the back of the room was not exactly the ideal place for a pair like Don and Rate. Upon someone's suggestion, they began to play Simon says: thumbs up or thumbs down. As the game progressed, they began to laugh when someone was caught moving his thumbs when "Simon" hadn't preceded the order. Finally, they became noisy enough to gain the attention of the teacher. Mrs. Ingersoll gave them a withering look and caustically asked, "And just what are you three boys celebrating?"

"The Fourth of July," piped up Don with an impish look.

It seemed Don was always one to have a ready answer that on more than one occasion was to get him into trouble. He also looked like he enjoyed misbehaving, the devil danced in his eyes. Rate was the one with the wide-eyed innocent expression.

The students laughed. Mrs. Ingersoll didn't even crack a smile. She stalked to where the boys sat, yanked Burl out of his seat, and shook him until he was afraid his head was going to fly off. With no uncertain admonitions, she sat him back in his desk and grabbed

Don. After shaking him severely, and at the same time berating him for his actions, she shoved him back down. It was Rate's turn.

Now, Rate had watched the process thus far with quite some trepidation. He had often provoked a teacher, but he had never had one get violent with him before. He wasn't about to be shook like a dirty dust mop. As she grabbed him, he clutched the desk with both hands. She grabbed his arm, then his shirt, and his heart sank as all four buttons went popping off. She pried the first hand loose, and as she began to work on the other, he held on tenaciously with the first hand again. Finally, she could see that this was getting her exactly nowhere, and she could hear the twittering of laughter as the other students watched with interest. Suddenly, she stopped.

"Frankie, go fetch me a willow switch from the patch across the road." "Yes, ma'am," said Frankie Swarthout as he left his seat and headed out the door.

"All of you have work to do, and this is no concern of yours, so get busy."

All eyes returned to their books. Ralph was the only one who eyed the teacher. Cripes! If she gave him a licking, that meant he'd get one from Pa. The schoolmarm didn't frighten him, but he certainly didn't relish the thought of Pa trouncing him. He still remembered the last time Pa had licked him. Golly, here came Frankie. Well, he conceded, he supposed he had sort of brought it on himself.

Frankie gave Mrs. Ingersoll the switch and hastily sat down.

"Ralph, will you stand up and take your switching?"

Rate eyed her and shook his head. She raised the willow whip, aimed at his shoulders, and struck! Ralph ducked. The switch hit the desktop— and broke into several pieces. Frankie had done as he was bidden, but he had also cut the switch very carefully about every six inches in a circular motion so that only a small amount of wood held the switch together; thus, at the first whack, the willow had broken into pieces. Frankie had brought two switches. Mrs. Ingersoll picked up the second one, slowly bent it, whereupon it broke in the same fashion as the first. Without a word, she walked to the stove, opened the door, and tossed the pieces into the firepot, stood a moment as they caught fire, then closed the door with a bang.

If Ralph dawdled on his way home from school, it was with calculated intent. Golly, but Mrs. Ingersoll had been mad. Her face had turned a mottled red first and then more like a dull purple, and she had looked at him with venom in her eyes. Talk about if looks could kill—he'd be dead by now sure as shootin'. Then, she had drawn herself up very straight, to her full five foot six, and had marched stoically back to the front of the room, stood by her desk a moment, glared at the students as if inviting anyone to give hint of a smile or giggle, then calmly called the next class for recitation. A wave of relief had flooded the whole room.

Trouble was, no one knew if the matter was settled or not. Rate hadn't dared look around; he had ignored Don and Burl and got busy with his reading assignment. As usual, reading soon transported him from the world he lived in, and he had entered the pages of the book—if not physically, at least spiritually. For the entire length of the story, he had heard no more of the noise of the classroom. When dismissal time came, he slipped from his seat as quietly and unobtrusively as possible, grabbed his lunch pail, coat, and hat, crossed the schoolyard, and headed down the road at a rather rapid pace. However, the nearer he got to home, the slower his steps became.

Gripes. He'd have to tell his parents what had happened; otherwise, he'd have no explanation for the missing buttons from his shirt. Good thing there hadn't been any more, or they'd have been gone too. As it was, the shirt only opened halfway down the front, and that only gapped a little, showing a smidgen of his spring underwear underneath.

As he neared the driveway, he noticed a rig standing in the yard and recognized it. Worse luck! It belonged to his grandparents. How come they were back from South Lyon? As if it wasn't bad enough to have to explain to his parents, he was going to have his grandmother looking at him like the leader of the inquisition. Good heavens, this was some day!

He came quietly into the kitchen, put his dinner pail on the kitchen cabinet, and hung his coat by the door. Well, might as well get it over with. He squared his shoulders, pulled his shirt front together, and stepped into the dining room.

"Hello, Grandfather. Hello, Grandmother."

"Hello, Ralph," they replied.

"Goodness, Ralph, whatever happened to you? Have you been fighting again?"

"No, Ma, I haven't been fighting."

"Then, why are the buttons missing from your shirt?"

"Oh, that."

"Yes, that. Now, what have you been up to?"

Lovina eyed the boy sternly. Both Millie and Horatio watched the boy expectantly, no smile on their lips, but the crinkles around their eyes were deep, and the eyes shone.

Ralph scuffled his feet, looked down at the floor, heaved a sigh, and related his story, giving an accurate and concise account of what had happened. When he reached the part where the teacher had left him to return to the front of the schoolroom, his father interrupted.

"You mean she never actually whipped you?"

"No, Pa. I ducked, and she hit the desk 'stead of me. It made her madder'n a wet hen 'cause she knew what Frankie had done. She just let me alone. No, sir, she never walloped me at all."

"Lucky for you, boy. You do mind what I told you when you first begun school?"

"Yes, Pa. If I got a lickin' at school, I'd get another when I got home."

Millie nodded his assent.

Lovina and Miney did not seem to find the situation humorous; while neither of the men smiled, their features remained stern, the crinkles by the brown eyes were there, and the eyes showed merriment. Obviously, they viewed this infraction with a different viewpoint than their wives. Of course, it wasn't a man's job to replace the torn-off buttons either.

"There are times when the lad puts me in mind of when Millie and John were boys. Their clothes were always torn, buttons always missing, they attracted dirt like sugar does flies, and were always fighting with someone over something. Rate often found it comical," she accused.

"Now, Vine, did I ever uphold their antics even though they were just being normal boys? And many's the time they got a whipping over some mischief or for slacking off on their work."

"Well, I'd like for my grandson to be less trouble. I'd not wish all that on any woman."

Mina couldn't believe her ears. Her mother-in-law was actually thinking kind thoughts of Miney. Wonders would never cease. 'Course she knew Millie and John had been a handful to raise. Most of their mischief, Millie often said, was just good, clean fun, and they never hurt anyone. Guess Father had taken a dim view of some things because it was common knowledge that he had used the buggy whip on more than one occasion.

Millie had told more than once about getting a whipping, and how he would try to work himself closer to his father so he'd get struck with the part of the whip that was thicker because it didn't sting as much. His father would say, "Stand out there, boy, and take your licking." For sure, Father Setterington had been a stern father. Miney was glad Millie had never been that harsh with Ralph even if the boy did seem to be forever getting into trouble.

Rate watched his grandmother in wonderment as she talked. So Pa and Uncle John had torn their clothes too. The way Ma talked sometimes, he had thought he was the only boy who ever got dirty or had accidents with his clothes. Gosh, he wondered what kind of mischief Pa had got into. Sometimes, Pa liked to tell stories about when he was young, so Rate made up his mind to ask Pa about it. Maybe Pa had been just an ordinary boy after all.

It was a lovely, Saturday afternoon, warm and sunny, with the slightest of breezes gently rippling the leaves on the trees. It was the kind of day that gave a young lad itchy feet, the wanderlust, the desire to roam the meadows in search of a woodchuck hole; wander along the river and maybe observe a kingfisher sitting on a limb that stretched out over the water, patiently waiting for some unwary fish to swim by and then *whoosh!* down into the water it would plummet and up it would come with a fish in its beak. Yessir, there were just any amount of things Rate would have liked to be doing, but here he sat politely listening to the grown-ups' conversation while his thoughts wandered. The only consolation was that Blanche didn't look as if she was enjoying herself either.

Aunt Ruby, Uncle Mac, Grandmother and Grandfather, and, of course, Lois were visiting; Rate got pretty fed up with hearing Grandmother tell of the "darling" way Lois did this and that. She looked like any little girl to him, and she couldn't even walk alone, although Grandmother had been quick to show off how the child would take several steps to get to her grandmother, but would simply refuse to attempt walking to anyone else, even her own mother. Lovina fairly burst with pride.

Ralph wondered how it made Blanche feel not to be the apple of Grandmother's eye anymore. 'Course Grandmother didn't treat him any differently. Although there were numerous occasions when he remembered her being particularly kind, for the most part, she had pretty much ignored his existence. It was kinda funny seeing Blanche look so bored and Grandmother so wrapped up in Lois she had scarcely replied to something Blanche had told her.

Millie spoke of the two foals, a colt and a filly, born the first of the month. As usual, he wanted his father to look them over and give his opinion of the two youngsters. It was decided that the entire group would go along—all except Lois and Ralph.

"Here, Ralph, we'll only be gone a few minutes, and you can just watch Lois for us."

With that admonition, Ruby plunked Lois on Ralph's lap.

"But, Aunt Ruby, what if she cries?"

"Walk around with her, and she'll be quiet until we get back."

As the group trooped out of the house, Rate looked at Lois with misgivings. The child returned his stare, then broke into gurgles of delight as she grabbed his nose; next she latched onto the lock of hair that had fallen onto his forehead. Babies! Golly, they were a nuisance. He hoisted her into his arms and walked over by the door. Lois poked an exploratory finger into his ear, pounded on his cheek with a pudgy hand, and kicked and squirmed.

After a short period, Ralph figured the group had been gone long enough. He watched as they stood by the fence watching the mares and their foals. What on earth was taking so long? Bet if Lois started crying, they'd be back in a hurry. Ralph sat her on the floor hoping she'd cry; she just gurgled and crawled over to pull herself up to a chair. Guess that didn't work. He picked her up once again. Then, a secretive grin appeared. Lois started to wail loud and long. Rate had pinched her.

"Ralph," called Aunt Ruby, "what is wrong?"

"Don't know. She just started crying." He pinched her again. "See, I'm walking her, and she still cries."

Ruby hurried to the house followed by Lovina. Lois calmed as soon as Ruby took her; two big tears rolled down her fair cheeks as she looked accusingly at Ralph. Rate gave her his most innocent look. Sure was a good thing she couldn't talk, Rate thought as Ruby cuddled her child.

Blanche came close and hissed, "Bet you did something on purpose. Bet you pinched her just 'cause you didn't like taking care of her. Aren't you ashamed?"

"Did no such thing," came the reply. "Can't help it if she doesn't like me, can I?"

Blanche shook her head and moved off. Sure was odd that Lois had cried when she was such a good-natured baby. That Ralph, she knew he'd done something even if he never would admit it.

*****

Rate had been listening to students in the seventh and eighth grade as they recited some poetry for reading class. Mrs. Ingersoll had been more than a little upset when a few of the students were not able to recite the stanza without considerable help. She scolded and impressed upon them they would have to recite again tomorrow, and she expected a great improvement. The selection was canto 6, stanza 1 from *The Lay of the Last Minstrel* by Sir Walter Scott; perhaps a little difficult, but it contained such a good message.

At recess time, Ralph edged up to the teacher's desk. "Mrs. Ingersoll."

"Yes, Ralph. What is it?"

"You know that poem the older ones is learning. I can say it."

"You can what?"

"I can repeat all of it."

The teacher viewed him with skepticism.

"Ralph, do you mean you can recite the entire stanza?"

"Ever bit."

"How did you learn it?"

"I listened while the others was sayin' it. Want me to show you?"

"Land's sakes. That's a lot for a third grader, but if you're sure you can do it, how would you like to recite it to everyone after recess? That ought to put some of the older ones to shame."

Ralph grinned. "I'd like it fine."

Recess time over, the students back in their seats, but instead of calling the usual class, Mrs. Ingersoll spoke to all the students.

"Some of you have been complaining about your piece to memorize. Well, we have someone who had memorized the selection because he wanted to. Ralph, will you say it now?"

Ralph flashed a smile, slid out of his seat, and walked to the front of the classroom. There, he recited clearly and with much more expression than the teacher had thought possible:

Breathes there the man, with soul so
    dead,
Who never to himself hath said,
    This is my own, my native land!

Whose heart hath ne'er within him
    burn'd
As home his footsteps he hath turn'd,
    From wandering on a foreign strand?
If such there breathe, go, mark him well;
For him no minstrel raptures swell;
High though his titles, proud his name,
Boundless his wealth as wish can claim,—
Despite those titles, power, and pelf,
The wretch, concentred all in self,
Living, shall forfeit fair renown,
And, doubly dying, shall go down
To the vile dust, from whence he sprung,
Unwept, unhonour'd, and unsung.

*****

Ralph knew that sometime this summer the mail would be delivered to a mailbox in front of their house instead of being left up on the corner. Couldn't happen any too soon to suit him. During the summer months, when the weather was good, Blanche often got the mail. Some days, they both watched to see if the mailman, Will Letts, stopped at the corner, and then they sometimes raced to see who could get there first. Blanche always liked to go on the day the *Toledo Blade*, a weekly newspaper, was delivered since she was becoming interested in world affairs. He rather liked having her get the mail and only raced her to tease. Still, if it was rainy, Blanche could never take a turn then, and since Pa had told him it was his job, there was no question as to who traipsed through the rain to the corner and back.

Then, another thing. Blanche was forever getting him into trouble. Pa blamed him for everything whether it was something he did or not. Like day before yesterday. Blanche had been the one to go get the mail. Well, when Pa came home from town, he had found a letter on the road that she had dropped. It had never occurred to Millie to ask who had gone for the mail that day, he simply assumed it had been Ralph and had berated him for being so careless. What had really angered Ralph was that he was almost certain Blanche had heard the whole thing, yet she had not come forward to admit her guilt. Perhaps he was being unfair to his sister. The way Pa always took Blanche's part in every way, he bet Pa wouldn't have believed her anyway. Rate had known there was no use trying to defend himself because Pa wouldn't have believed him, and then he would have been in trouble for lying. Wonder just why Pa always thought everything was his fault?

Sometimes, when the windmill didn't run, water for the livestock had to be pumped by hand. Rate would do his turn, but Blanche often conveniently forgot her turn; then, Pa always yelled at Ralph to get out there and finish the job. Sometimes, lately, Pa was even worse than Ma. At least Ma yelled at Blanche on occasion; and when they were younger, he had seen Blanche get her legs switched for being sassy. Seems the older he got, the more Pa favored Blanche. He just wished he could figure out why.

Miney had just received a disturbing letter from Ettie. In fact, she sat with the letter in her hand and cried bitter tears. She washed her face and eyes with cold water, but the eyes were still red and the lids swollen. She was in control of herself now, so she reread the letter.

"My dearest sister," it began. "By the time you receive this, I might very well be dead. The child is due any day now, and, Miney, I am so huge, I know I'll never be able to have this baby. George tries to be cheerful, but even he is worried although he tries desperately not to show it. I can hardly get around, and it is difficult for me to get out of a rocker without help.

"I want you to know that you have been a good sister. Sometimes, I wish we had not lived so far apart and could have seen more of each other. Our children never really knew one another.

"I hope the baby dies with me. It would be a hard world for a baby to grow up without a mother, although George would no doubt marry again if there was a child. If not, he assures me he will live alone—says he wants no other woman.

"I must write to Mary and Lorin as well. God bless you, Miney, and know that I have cared."

It was signed, "Your loving sister, Ettie." The letter was dated June 12, 1902.

Five days later, Miney received a telegram:

Ettie and baby died this morning.

Funeral Wednesday. Wire if coming. George.

Mina could not keep back the flood of tears. Ettie was her own sister, and while somewhat different in many ways, they had got on well as children. Perhaps it was the way Ettie had died that bothered Miney the most. She felt resentment toward her brother-in-law. Ettie was just too old to have been in the family way, and the blame for that was certainly to be laid at George's doorstep. She was glad her mother had not lived to see this day. 'Course, Ma had been forty-one when Miney was born, so Ma might have looked at the situation differently. From what little her mother had ever said about childbearing, Miney assumed her mother had had little, if any, trouble bearing children. She guessed some women were just luckier than others. Miney recalled with displeasure the intense pain she had borne while giving birth to Blanche, and it had been nearly as bad for Ralph. She fervently hoped she would not get in the family way again. What a horrible thought! She'd just view her feelings to Millie and impress upon him that she did not want to be in Ettie's shoes.

Goodness, there was always something for a woman to worry about. Mina had felt she was getting beyond the childbearing years, but Ettie was a dire reminder this was not so. A woman's lot certainly was a sorry one much of the time. Perhaps if she asked

God not to have any more children, He would heed her prayers. It wouldn't hurt to ask, and she would start this very night.

Miney and Lorin were to take the train to Traverse City. Just before she left, Miney decided to check her money for train fare, which she had tied up in a handkerchief. She had already done this several times. The handkerchief was tucked in the bodice of her gown; only this time, there was no handkerchief and no money. Miney began a frantic search of the house. She enlisted Millie's help, and even the children began a rather haphazard search.

"Millie," she cried, "whatever will I do if I can't find it? I don't have enough money left for another ticket."

"Don't fret. It has to be here somewheres. I've got a little change, so I think we can scrape up enough for your ticket. Wouldn't give you any extree though. If Pa was here, we could get it from him."

"I'd sooner not go than borrow money from him," muttered Miney.

Millie chose to overlook that remark. He knew Miney often resented his relationship with his parents; she just never acknowledged that both Ma and Pa could be mighty generous people. Miney just never seemed to understand.

"Miney, you're running around like a chicken with its head cut off. Now, start by retracing your steps. Just what did you do after you put the money in the handkerchief?"

Miney stopped and thought.

"Well, I sat in front of the dresser and combed and braided my hair."

They looked under the dresser. Nothing.

"I went into the kitchen to see if the meat on the stove had enough water on it."

They even looked under the stove—to no avail.

"Oh, yes, I went out to get a pail of water."

A glance out the door showed nothing. However, the hired man went on out the door. There were wide planks covering the space between the house and the well curb. Charlie, playing a hunch, started moving the planks and saw the bit of white cloth standing out against the moist dark earth. Sure enough, it was the missing handkerchief with money intact.

"Now, Miney, are you ready to go? The sooner you get your ticket bought, the better. Think we should let Lorin carry your money and ticket for you?" Millie laughed.

"Don't be funny," snapped Miney.

"Well, you haven't been doing so good keeping track of it."

"Never mind. I'm ready to go."

Miney was slightly miffed. She had voiced her thoughts to Millie regarding her sister's death, and although he had said very little, she knew he did not share her sentiments. He had even had the audacity to ask her if she wasn't always the one who said we don't necessarily understand why the Lord does things the way He does. Of course, she had to admit this was so. Then, he had asked what made her think this was not the Lord's doing. She had no answer. When presented in this fashion, to say it was not the Lord's work made it seem as if her faith was not strong.

Miney truly did believe the Bible, and it was only her personal loss that had given her moments of doubt. She knew in her heart God had His reasons, even if she could not understand. Perhaps someday she would be enlightened.

*****

Blanche sat at the piano in the parlor dutifully practicing her lesson. Mina had pestered Millie to buy them a piano instead of the organ they had had when they were first married just so Blanche could be given lessons. Why, Mina had been playing the organ when the most difficult part had been to pump it because her legs were hardly long enough to reach. She had taken readily to music and had hoped her aptitude would be passed on to her daughter. However, Miney was beginning to have her doubts. She had been giving Blanche lessons for some time now, yet Blanche's progress seemed to be incredibly slow. Miney had other students who had started after Blanche and were much further in their book than Blanche. Goodness, that was a sour chord!

"Blanche! Blanche, you made a mistake. Can't you hear that it doesn't sound right?"

"I know, Ma, I just didn't feel like correcting it."

"If I've told you once, I've told you a dozen times, it only makes it worse if you don't take time to correct your mistakes. Now, start that last piece over."

"Oh, Ma, do I have to? I've already practiced over twenty minutes, and I'm not nearly through with all that you gave me for a lesson."

"It won't hurt to go over the half hour."

Mina came into the parlor wiping her hands on her apron.

"Now, try it again. Take it a little slower, and I'm sure you can play it right," cajoled Miney.

Blanche started the piece once again. A few measures later, her finger hit a wrong note.

"Blanche, you forgot you have two flats in the signature, not just one. Goodness, child, I just don't believe you keep your mind on your practicing."

"I try, Ma. I just don't know why my fingers always hit the wrong keys."

With that admission, she burst into tears. Miney gathered her daughter into her arms to comfort her.

"Now, now, it isn't worth tears. If we move into town, I'm going to speak to Mabel Wooley. Perhaps you would do better if you had someone else for a teacher. How would you like that?"

"I don't know. I just don't think I was meant to play the piano."

"Nonsense. Why, when I was your age, I played piano for church services for both the Methodist and the Baptist Church. They had their services at different hours, so it was an easy matter to play for the Methodist service then go across the street for the Baptist service. Once in a while, if the minister took too long for his sermon, I'd nearly be late." She chuckled. "If I could do it, so can you."

"Ma, it just isn't in me. But I'll try just to please you."

"That's my girl. One of these days you'll find that all of a sudden, it will come much easier. Just you wait and see."

The next afternoon, Mina called up the stairsteps, "Blanche, come down here. Pa just brought a package for you from the post office."

"What is it, Ma?"

"That's for you to find out. It's from your uncle George in Traverse City."

There it was, a package addressed to her in her uncle George's beautiful writing with his name as the sender. She eyed the package in awe. She'd never had anything sent to her through the mail before except cards or letters, and not many of them.

"Aren't you going to open it?" asked Miney.

"Yes, of course. Oh dear, my fingers are all thumbs," Blanche exclaimed as she tore at the wrappings. She managed to get them off, revealing a box, which gave her further difficulty.

"Ma, you do it. I can't seem to get the top off."

"Here, child. If you weren't so anxious, it would help."

In the box nestled in a bed of cotton was a lady's gold watch.

"Isn't it lovely? Look, Ma, it has a long chain to wear around my neck. It is just beautiful."

"It's Ettie's watch. George gave it to her before they were married."

"You mean this belonged to Aunt Ettie?"

"Here, there's a letter too," put in Millie. "Maybe Doc explains it in there."

Blanche read the letter. Before her death, Ettie Smith Curtis had expressed the wish that Blanche, her favorite niece, be given her watch since it had great sentimental value. She asked that Miney keep the watch for Blanche until she was fifteen, at which age Ettie felt the girl would be capable of appreciating so valuable a gift. George was only too happy to honor his wife's last request.

Aunt Ettie had passed away in June; however, Blanche had never cared much for her aunt, so she had not really grieved her passing. She had once heard someone describe Ettie as a "spineless creature." Blanche felt the words were apt and had forever after thought of Ettie in that way. She remembered the time before she started school when she, Ma, and Ralph had gone to Traverse City to visit them. Uncle George had been a doctor then except Aunt Ettie had complained and complained, first about him being gone so much—especially at night when she was scared to death to stay alone—then about the long hours he worked, so he had been studying law on the side. Blanche guessed Aunt Ettie had complained less since Uncle George had opened a law office and kept regular hours; although she still complained about her health, which everyone felt was mostly in her head.

Blanche had liked Uncle Doc. George W. Curtis, better known as Doc to his old friends, was a promising attorney in Traverse City, and she had always been a little proud to let other playmates know that she had an uncle who was a lawyer. Now, it made her feel just a little bit ashamed of herself that while she had thought so little of Aunt Ettie, her aunt had sent her a prized possession. It made Blanche feel rather humble for a moment. Then, the terms of the gift registered in her mind.

"But, Ma, does that mean I can't wear it until I'm fifteen? That's… that's two whole years from now."

"That's what George's letter says. I'm afraid we must respect the wishes of the deceased. We'll just put it away until you're older."

That beautiful gold watch in that beautiful case. It looked alike on both sides until you pressed the release to open the front. Aunt Ettie would be just the one to think she wasn't old enough to take care of something of value. Now, Aunt Mary would have been different. Bet Uncle Doc hadn't had anything to say about it either. He'd probably been too upset over knowing Aunt Ettie was dying to give it much thought, especially since Ma somehow believed it was Uncle Doc's fault his wife had died. Well, two years was better than ten. She looked at the watch once more, returned it to the box, gave the box to her mother, and didn't mention it again. Of course, she wrote to Uncle Doc to thank him, but it was as if the watch had never existed. However, she and her uncle would keep up a correspondence until his death.

Don and Burl Sherman came over to spend the afternoon with Ralph. They had been back to the creek for a while, played catch for a while, and had ended up in the barn dangling from the hay ropes and walking the beams.

Later, no one was sure whose idea it was to hitch up the two yearling calves that were tied on the barn floor. The boys worked with a will using bits of a leather driving harness and rope to fashion harnesses of sorts. Finally, all was in readiness, and they opened the big barn doors to let the calves out. Don was driving.

Burl had taken one calf by the head while Rate had the other. They managed to get them outside with no problem. Then, all hell broke loose. Both calves began to kick and jump, one tried to turn around to face Don while the other bounded straight ahead. Neither Burl nor Ralph could get close enough to grab their heads as the two calves pulled and jerked Don along every way for Sunday. It seemed that the more the boys tried to calm them down, the more they kicked, and the more entangled they became in the hastily completed harness.

"Rate, whyn't you get ahold o' their heads?" yelled Don.

"Ha! Like to see you manage. Why are you lettin"em drag you?"

"I've got my feet braced. Burl, can't you help?"

"What am I supposed to do? I'm not gonna get kicked ifn I can help it."

"Well, somebody do something. I'm not gonna be able to hold 'em much longer."

"Hang on, Curly. I think they're getting tired," said Ralph as he grabbed the halter of one.

It was true, the initial fervor was dwindling as the calves' sides heaved, attesting to their exertion. Then, came the summons.

"Rate! Come here," commanded Millie from near the woodshed.

"We've gone and done it now," Rate confided to his companions. "I didn't know Pa was around. He sure sounded mad."

"We're goin' home," said Don. "He never yelled for us to come with you. Hope you don't get a lickin'."

"Me too."

Ralph managed to get the calves back into the barn while Don and Burl skedaddled cross-lots for home.

"You want me, Pa?"

"Called you, didn't I?"

"Yessir."

"Guess you know what you got coming." "Reckon so," mumbled Ralph.

"Speak up, boy. What have you got coming?"

"A lickin', I 'spect. But, Pa—"

"No excuses. Rate, you should have known better. Since you didn't, I'll give you something so's you won't be likely to forget. Wouldn't want you to get into the same mischief twice."

With that, Millie proceeded to use a barrel stave to give Ralph his third and final whipping. As to whether he deserved others as time went by, there might have been a difference of opinion. In all probability, his mother could have cited numerous occasions when she felt a licking was warranted. However, this final whipping was not one he was to forget very readily.

Blanche was doing the dusting as usual. Miney normally did the sweeping, so that left the dusting up to Blanche. She used the turkey wing to dust the intricately carved legs of the marble-top table; she used the dustcloth on the top. Next, she moved into the spare bedroom. Here, she ran her cloth along the exposed part of the dresser. They only took the dresser scarfs off on Fridays when they did the weekly cleaning. The daily dusting was more of a hit-or-miss job. Blanche paused before a picture that had two long peacock feathers crossed above the frame. They were so pretty, the colors varied and beautiful.

She turned and went out to the kitchen where her mother was just taking up a dustpan of dirt.

"Ma, where'd you get those peacock feathers you're so choice about?"

"Mrs. Stafford gave those to me several years ago."

"Did the Staffords have peacocks?"

"They did. Said they were better than a watchdog to let you know if someone strange was around. I used to watch for them when we drove by, always hoping to catch one with its tail spread. They are so beautiful with the sun glinting on the various colors. Once in a while, they'd be sitting on the peak of the barn."

"Did they raise them?"

"Sometimes. Guess they aren't all that easy to raise. Anyway, I was talking to Mrs. Stafford one day, telling her how much I admired her birds, and she up and gave me those two feathers. I suppose the colors will fade in time, but they are certainly gorgeous now."

"They are that. Wish we had some peacocks."

"Blanche, your father would think I had lost my senses if I was to suggest such a thing." Miney laughed.

"Why?"

"Well, he's not one to keep something that doesn't earn its keep. 'Course I guess way back in history, royalty used to eat peacocks, but I'm sure I could never kill one to eat."

Blanche digested this as she went back to finish her dusting. Yes, she guessed Ma was right. Pa just wasn't one to go in for something frivolous, and she was sure he'd feel peacocks were definitely frivolous.

It was Saturday, and the family was just finishing breakfast when Millie turned to his young son.

"Rate, I've got a job for you this morning."

"What is it, Pa?"

"Heard in town yesterday that old man Cobb has a heifer calf for sale. You can go over there this morning, and if you can get it for a reasonable price, buy it."

"What's a reasonable price?"

"As little as he's willing to take."

Ralph knew better than to question his father further. Big lot of help that answer had been. Well, Pa would have to give him some money, so he guessed he'd just try and buy the calf for less than what Pa gave him.

When Ralph came to leave, Millie gave his son ten dollars with the admonition that he not spend any more than he had to.

Rate kept going over and over in his mind what he would say to Mr. Cobb. Nothing seemed to sound just right. He wanted to do a good job so his father would be proud of him. He knew for certain if he gave more than Pa figured the calf was worth, Pa would be quick enough to tell him about it.

When he arrived at the Cobb farm east of Elsie, Arthur recognized him right off. They tethered the horse and went to the barn to look at the calf.

"How much you askin', Mr. Cobb?"

"Wal now, I did reckon she'd be wuth maybe ten dollars, but since you're Millie's son, I guess I could take as little as eight."

"I dunno, Mr. Cobb. She seems kinda scrawny to me. I doubt she's worth more'n five," Rate said with much more bravado than he felt.

"Rate, you just look her over good. See how deep the body is. She'll make a fine cow. How about seven?"

"Mr. Cobb, I still think she's a mite small. She may make a good looking cow, but she sure looks to be on the small side. No, sir, Mr. Cobb, I don't figger she's worth no more than six," Rate said with a determined note in his voice.

The boy watched the older man, almost holding his breath, waiting for the older man's answer. Mr. Cobb took off his hat, scratched his head, looked at the calf as if this was indeed a monumental decision.

"Don't think she's wuth seven, huh? Got the cash, was I to take six?"

"Oh, yessir, right here in my pocket."

"You drive a hard bargain, mind you, and I'm not saying she ain't wuth the seven, but I don't want to monkey with feedin' her, so I guess you've bought yourself a calf."

Whew! Rate heaved a sigh of relief as he dug into his trouser pocket for the six dollars. Boy, that was four less than Pa had given him, so Pa sure oughta be pleased.

However, when Ralph got the calf home, Millie looked it over critically and only nodded when Ralph explained that Mr. Cobb had come down to six dollars.

"Wouldn't take five?"

"No, Pa, I didn't think he was even gonna let her go for six. Not at first anyway."

Millie made no further comment as he tied the calf on the barn floor.

He told Ralph to bed her down and moved off to finish his chores.

Ralph tried hard not to show his disappointment. He had wanted so badly to get a word of praise from his father. For some unknown reason, Millie always found it impossible to praise Ralph for anything.

Later that night, Millie related the event to Miney.

"By golly, Miney, the lad's got horse sense. I'd have given eight for that calf, but he got it for six. He's a right sharp one when it comes to knowin' his livestock. He'll do all right for himself, he will."

Millie never realized how much good it would have done a small boy to have heard these words of praise.

*****

Rain dripped from the eaves; the leaves of the cottonwood hung mournfully low, clasping droplets that became glowing crystals in the sun. Ralph gazed idly out the window absently rubbing Bruno's ears. The dog sensed his master's preoccupation, so he whined and moved a little closer with his head resting on Rate's knee. Rate was so completely lost in thought he scarcely noticed the dog. Jeepers, he'd heard Ma and Pa talking. They might move to town for the winter since Blanche didn't have a place to stay anymore.

Girls were one heck of a lot of bother. Blanche couldn't drive to town all year, yet Pa could make the trip to the farm twice a day, and Rate knew there would be plenty of times he'd have to accompany his father. That wasn't the worst part. It meant he'd have to go to town to school too, and that meant not having Curly and Rollie to play with.

Rate was right. Millie and Mina decided that it would be too much to expect Blanche to drive to school each day when the weather got bad. Since they would be moving the first of November, they decided there was no sense in letting Ralph start in at Stafford. He could just go to Elsie with Blanche.

Little did either Miney or Millie realize the resentment this would cause. Ralph disliked the idea of leaving his friends. On top of that, he resented the fact that everyone, including Blanche, accepted the fact that Rate assume all responsibility for caring for the horse. They still had milk to take to the creamery although they only took their own. Blanche had been perfectly capable of handling the work last spring; Rate wondered why all of a sudden it became too difficult for her to do.

Blanche usually got off down town while he continued on to the creamery by himself. When it was time to go home, she managed to talk to a girlfriend or two until Rate had the horse hitched up to the wagon or buggy, whichever they were driving for the day. Wouldn't do any good to say something to Pa or Ma because they would just tell him it wasn't a woman's work. Things sure did seem unfair at times.

Rate missed seeing Curly although he quickly made new friends. Bud Grell, who was older, even let Rate learn to ride his bike at recess time. Naw, he liked his new friends all right, only he did wish he could see more of Curly. Perhaps he missed the mischief they had gotten into together. Curly always had a big mouth, and it did get him into trouble, but Ralph had usually thought it funny even if it involved him and he had had to share the punishment.

Mostly, he resented that their whole world must revolve around Blanche. He didn't realize that Blanche never asked for all this adulation, and that at times, she found it somewhat stifling. He just knew that more and more it became apparent his parents loved Blanche and seemingly only tolerated him. Yet, he and Pa did get along. They teased one another, and Pa never really got mad at him. Still, the older they got, the more Millie favored his daughter. Sure was hard to figger out.

Pa often was quite vociferous in his opinion that his parents made fools of themselves catering to Ruby. It always seemed that Pa resented the fact that Ruby was the favorite, yet it was sure enough easy to see Blanche was Pa's favorite. Just didn't seem fair. If Pa could criticize his own parents for their behavior toward a daughter, then why was he doing the exact same thing? The Setterington men were somehow all very similar.

Rate had already driven to where the milk had been unloaded. The big arms had come out, taken the milk can, stopped for the scales, and then dumped it into a huge vat. Now, he pulled ahead and around the corner of the building to pick up the whey. Just ahead of him were the Garrett twins, Mabel and Muriel. They looked back and waved, so he rather nonchalantly waved back. The thought flitted across his mind that these two girls weren't as old as Blanche, and they didn't seem to mind hauling milk. In fact, they had a ready smile for everyone. He didn't know them well enough yet to tell them apart because they were identical twins.

When he finally pulled up to the pump for his portion of whey, Sam Packingham stumped over, and being in a particularly affable mood, he was in no hurry to get on with his job of pumping the hot whey into the milk can.

"Wal now, Rate, I seen you makin' sheep's eyes at those two purty gals. Ain'tcha a little young fur gal friends?"

"I only waved 'cause they did. Haven't known 'em long," he explained.

"Sure. I seen 'em tryin' to catch your attention. Didn't see you ignorin''em any. 'Course they's mighty nice gals. Don't do no harm to start lookin' early."

"I'm not looking," came the patient elucidation. "I had to be polite, didn't I?"

"'Course you did, boy. I seen you wuz jest bein' perlite." He winked suggestively at Ralph while he turned to the pump, held the canvas tube over the milk can, and methodically worked the old wooden pump.

Now, what was wrong with returning the girls' waves? Sam was just makin' a mountain out of a molehill. Besides, he was sure the girls were at least two grades ahead of him. Why would Sam think he'd be interested in girls anyhow? Sam was a funny old coot; the way he stumped around on his peg leg always made it seem as if he was in a terrible rush. Blanche always thought him grumpy, but he didn't seem that way to Ralph.

Each day for several days, the Garrett girls were just a rig or two ahead of Ralph at the cheese factory. Just like clockwork, Sam took time to comment about Ralph and his girlfriends.

"Rate, ain't no one never told you they's a law again' havin' two wimmen? Bein's that's so, which one are ya gonna take, Mabel or Muriel? 'Course, not many could tell the diffrunce anyhow." He laughed.

Ralph stared straight ahead at his horse's ears. He'd simply not give that old man the satisfaction of knowing all these jibes bothered him. He'd just ignore him, that's what he'd do.

He was soon to learn that a man like Sam was hard to ignore. He was like a hound on a hot scent; he knew he was bothering the lad, so he continued the attack.

"Why, Rate, you mean you can't make up yore mind? Want me to give you a hint on how to choose?"

"Would you hurry up and give me my whey? You're going to make me late for school."

"Couldn't have that, now could we?"

Sam laughed and soon finished his job. Rate was glad to get away from there. He was sure some of the other farmers could hear what Sam had to say. How embarrassing.

The next morning, Ralph was in no mood to hear any more of Sam's words of wisdom. Drat it all, he was tired of being teased about girls. An idea came to mind. Just this once, he'd go home without any whey; he'd tell Pa that he'd been kinda far back in line, and they ran out of whey before they got to him. He knew it wasn't right to lie, but just this once he felt it might be justified. After all, he'd taken all the guff he was going to from that old man.

Although Rate was somewhat apprehensive when he told his father the little white lie, it worked, and Millie just nodded his head in acknowledgment and said nothing. This was not the last time Ralph was to come home without stopping to get any whey. If Millie ever surmised that his son was not being completely honest, he never let it be known.

Ralph did not know how to cope with being teased about girls. In the first place, he hadn't thought of liking girls because they were girls—he just liked them because he could always think of something to do to vex them. Had Sam chosen to pick on Ralph about anything else, he would have found a quick mind, with a parry and riposte for any attack. The old Civil War veteran took much delight in watching the youth squirm, and he enjoyed it even more when a deepening red blush crept over the lad's face.

Come November, before snow flew, the family moved into Grandma Smith's house. Millie drove back and forth to the farm to do chores. After school, Ralph was expected to go with his father, and often on Saturdays, they spent most of the day at the farm. Now, Ralph saw less of Curly than before. Still, it was rather nice not to have chores to do mornings before he went to school. Well, at least not many. He had to go across the street to the barn and take care of the two driving horses, but that didn't take long. Guess living in town wasn't all bad.

However, Ralph did look forward to spring since he knew they would once again move back to the farm. During the summer, he would have Curly and Rollie for companions. No matter how well he got on with his new friends, no one could quite replace Curly Sherman; theirs was indeed a lasting friendship.

CHAPTER 8

B lanche was upstairs in her room. Ma had gone to visit Aunt Lorin, and Ralph was heaven knew where, so just she and Pa were home. Because Pa was seldom one for carrying on much of

a conversation, she had taken the book she was reading to her room.

She heard the front door open and close and thought perhaps her mother had returned early. A few moments later, she laid her book aside to go downstairs to talk with Miney. As she reached the back stairway, she heard voices raised in anger coming from the sitting room. She recognized her father's tones immediately, and then she realized the other voice belonged to her uncle John.

She sneaked down the stairs to listen to what was being said. Eavesdropping was not something she should be doing, but she wondered why the brothers seemed so angry, why the raised voices; something had greatly agitated them both.

"I tell you, Millie, that damned old man hates my guts. He's never been a father to me, and you know it. He can rot in hell for all I care."

"Now, John, simmer down a bit. What's Pa done now?"

"I needed a loan, so I went to Pa. Where else should a man turn but to his father, especially when his old man's well-off? He just looked at me as though I was a piece of vermin and began lecturing me on what he calls my irresponsible ways."

"What in particular was he referring to?"

"How in hell should I know? Said he'd lent me enough money over the years to start out ten sons, and I'd managed to squander and mismanage ever red cent. Said I hadn't begun to repay the other loans. That ain't true, Millie."

John glared at his brother, daring him to disagree.

Blanche edged closer, wanting a better view, but not wanting to be discovered. She found her heart was pounding. Never had she seen Uncle John look so angry or Pa so distraught.

"John, be honest with yourself for once. You know you've traded more pieces of land than a dog's got fleas. Somehow, your trading never gains you one thin dime. You can't do a half-assed job of farming and make a go of it. Pa just wants you to put in six days of work each week like—"

"Like you, Milt? Go ahead and say it. You've always done just as the old man says. He says 'jump,' and you say 'how far?' How can you forget all those hidings with a horse whip? I suppose you'll tell me they were for our own good."

"In Pa's way, he thought they were. He was teaching us to accept our responsibilities in life. You asked for what you got. If you hadn't always slacked off on your share of the chores, Pa would never have got so mad. Own up to being on the lazy side, John."

John glared at his brother. He would've liked to have slammed his fist in Millie's face like when they were boys, but he thought better of it.

Sullenly, he muttered, "Still didn't give the old reprobate no right to whip me so. I always got it worse than you, an' you know it. Why in hell does he do everything for Mac and Ruby? Everyone knows Mac's not worth a hill of beans. Still, everything has to be done for Ruby. She's always been Ma's favorite. Ruby is perfect in their eyes. They get along with you because they can push you around. Me? I'm shit under their feet."

Millie tried in vain to reason with his brother. Just when he thought he had calmed John down, the man erupted all over again.

John's voice shook with emotion as he looked at his brother and said, "Milt, I could take that old man by the hair of the head, take a razor, and slit his throat from ear to ear with not an ounce of remorse." He shook his clenched fist as though holding his father's head and made a movement with his right hand as if drawing an imaginary razor across his father's throat.

Millie stared at his brother in disbelief. No words came for a moment; there was utter stillness in the room.

"By God, John, you have gone too far. I'll hear no more from you about Pa. Just get out of my house, and stay out until you've got some sense in your head. After all Pa's done for you, you could repay him like that? Ma's done her damnedest for you and Grace and the kids. Seems like you ought to be grateful for the help you've had. Think it over. When you can talk rationally, I'll talk to you. Not before." Millie had not raised his voice, but the tone was ominous.

John said nothing; he simply stomped out of the house. Millie leaned forward, his head in his hands, his mind in a turmoil. His own brother wanted their father dead. He couldn't think. He couldn't understand. Pa had been strict, but Pa had taught them honesty, responsibility, integrity, an honest day's work brought an honest day's pay.

How could John's warped mind speak of killing their father? Everyone knew John Setterington had a horrible temper, although it took a lot to rile him. Millie took comfort in believing John would simmer down and be sorry for his words. Still, it made him see John in a different light. It opened a breach that never completely healed.

Blanche wanted to comfort her father, but she didn't know how. Besides, she didn't want him to know she had overheard the conversation. She found she was trembling. Never would she feel any love for her uncle John. He had killed her love just as he wanted to kill her grandfather. Quietly, she slipped back upstairs to her room. Over and over she heard Uncle John's strident tones, and she shuddered.

Two nights later, Milford was gone for the evening, and Rate was spending the night with Don Sherman. Blanche and Mina were alone. Miney had her rocking chair drawn up close to the Rayo lamp on the table so the light would be good enough to do the crocheting she had started a few days ago. She was doing some wide lace for a pair of pillowcases to give as a Christmas present. She hadn't decided just who she was going to give them to, perhaps Ruby—although Ruby could be so uppity she might not think them good enough.

Blanche sat at the table engrossed in a book. In truth, her thoughts were elsewhere, and it had been several minutes since she had turned a page.

Finally, she spoke to her mother.

"Ma, did you know Uncle John came to see Pa when you were at Aunt Lorin's the other night?"

"Millie did mention it, although he never said what John wanted."

"I'm not sure what he wanted either, but he was awful mad about something. They didn't know I was in the house."

"Do you know what they were talking about?"

Blanche explained in detail what she had heard.

"Land's sakes. Oh, Blanche, I'm sorry you had to hear that."

"Me too. Honest, Ma, it just makes my stomach hurt. After all, Grandfather is Uncle John's father. How can he hate him so?"

"I don't know. I have never understood John with his shiftless ways. Well, that explains what was wrong with your father that night. I thought he acted strange. He said something about John being here, but he'd have been better off not to have come. When I questioned him about what he meant, he said something to the effect that his brother wasn't good for much and that he was the most unappreciative person he'd ever known. That was all I could get out of him. Goodness, Blanche, no wonder he was upset. To think that John could think such a thing, much less put it into words. God will certainly punish him for this."

"Ma, if Uncle John comes here again, do I have to be nice to him?"

"Yes, Blanche, you do. He is your uncle, and we are not to judge. God will do that. Oh my, I doubt if he will be back for some time. Your father will not forget easily, so I think he will avoid his brother whenever possible. Sometimes, down in his heart, I'm not sure your father always agrees with his father, but he has always had a great deal of respect for the man. Of course, Father Setterington has certainly been an astute businessman," she said grudgingly, "although I have always felt he was more than a little heartless."

Blanche digested this. She realized that sometimes Grandfather could be unreasonable in his demands and that he was terribly stubborn. 'Course, she felt Uncle John was equally stubborn. However, not to feel remorse if Grandfather died was unthinkable. Blanche loved and respected her grandfather. Besides, it was Grandmother who usually aroused her ire by her constant fault-finding. Grandfather never had a lot to say, but he was always pleasant to be around.

Blanche never forgot what she had heard John say, and she never found it in her heart to completely forgive him. She wasn't sure her father ever forgave him either.

*****

Christmas this year was a more exciting time since they had been invited to spend the day at South Lyon with Grandmother and Grandfather. Rate was glad of the diversion. He could remember the time he, Georgie, and Ma had gone by train to Traverse City to see Aunt Ettie and Uncle George, and the time when he and Blanche had gone to visit Aunt Ruby and Uncle Mac at Big Rapids; he could even remember going to Aunt Mary's in Chicago, and he had always enjoyed the train ride. True, going to South Lyon wasn't going to take very long, but even a short ride was better than none.

Besides, Christmas was the one time of year he enjoyed going to his grandmother's. She always fussed a lot more than Ma did. There was always plenty of oranges and bananas and fancy little candies that Grandmother so proudly made and all kinds of nuts to crack. For dessert, they always had what Grandmother called plum pudding, a steamed pudding with lots of raisins, although it tasted just like Ma's suet pudding. Anyway, Grandmother said hers was an old English recipe that came from Horatio's side of the family. Whether it was rightly named "suet" or "plum" pudding didn't matter much to Ralph since it was one of his very favorite desserts.

Grandmother served generous portions of the dark hot pudding with sweetened milk to pour over it. Just thinking of it made his mouth water, and he could almost taste it.

Since Grandfather was the town's only banker, he no longer wore full chin whiskers. Rate heard him say that the neatly trimmed Van Dyke was more in keeping with his new station in life. Personally, Ralph liked the transfiguration; he felt it gave his grandfather the distinguished look of an aristocrat. Horatio was tall, wiry, and by now his beard and the thinning hair was a steel gray, yet the eyes were as bold and black as they had ever been. Perhaps the lines at the corners of the eyes were more deeply set, the forehead was certainly higher, but Horatio carried his years well. The broad shoulders were still square, and there was no stoop; he stood as erect as a young man. Rate often watched his grandfather with a sort of inner pride.

Ralph had never really known his grandfather's brothers. He knew Uncle Albert and Uncle George had visited, but he scarcely remembered them. He only knew they had seemed large, much like Willie and John, who were Uncle Albert's boys. He did remember that the youngest brother, Uncle Vest, had come to see them. However, he just knew that his grandfather was the best-looking of the boys in the family. He had never seen any of Grandfather's sisters, although he assumed them to be large women. Blanche had always been tall for her age and broad-shouldered for a girl, and Ralph had heard Grandfather compare Blanche with his sisters.

He guessed Setteringtons were just special 'cause no one ever talked much about Grandmother's side of the family. Aunt Nan and Uncle Lem Bingham had once lived just west of the village limits on the north side of the road, and Aunt Nan was Grandmother's sister. He hadn't been all that old when Lem had sold the place to Grandfather. Rate remembered that was where he had seen his first and only barn raising.

Aunt Nan had died of cancer a few years ago. He remembered Uncle Lem as being a rather odd sort of person. He'd heard Pa say that was because Uncle Lem was a morphine addict. When Rate had questioned his father, Millie had told him that Lem Bingham had been hurt very seriously in an accident and had been given morphine for several weeks to make the pain bearable. The doctors had not realized that such prolonged use of the drug created a dependence on it, and the body developed a craving for the drug. They had been able to lessen the dosage, but Lem had never quite been able to forgo the withdrawal pain, so he had continued his use of the drug. Pa had told Ralph that before the accident, Lem had been a much different personality. Ralph had digested this bit of information resolving that if he ever got hurt, he'd tolerate the pain rather than be given drugs upon which he would become dependent for the rest of his life.

He knew a Lizzie Loynes called Grandmother *Aunt Vine*, so he supposed she was Grandmother's niece. He had asked Blanche about it one day, and Blanche had said that she sort of remembered Aunt Bet Loynes, who she guessed was Grandmother's sister. Blanche had told him that Grandmother never talked much about her family. Perhaps they weren't as prosperous as the Setteringtons, or perhaps Lovina just didn't get on well with them, neither Blanche nor Rate ever knew for certain.

Grandfather met them at the station with the cutter. As usual, he drove a highstepping, spirited team. Blanche and Miney clambered into the back seat and were snuggled under a beautiful horsehide robe, their hands shoved deeply into their muffs. Ralph asked to ride in front with the menfolk, who scoffed at such necessities to keep them warm. Even though the weather was in the lower teens, men had to be tough enough not to need coddling. When they moved away from the depot, Rate wished he could drive the team, but he was afraid to ask even though Grandfather looked in a particularly jovial mood, smiling and chatting with his son as though their arrival was indeed special.

If anyone wondered why John and Grace, with their five children, were not present for Christmas dinner, no one made mention of the fact. Grandmother was almost pleasant and found no fault with anyone, which Ralph felt must have set some sort of record. She played a great deal with Lois, so it was easy to see that there was now someone in her life who mattered more than Blanche. Well, perhaps it was only because Lois was still a baby, and Lovina did love babies—especially baby girls.

It was late March when Milford and his family moved back to the farm. Now that Ralph and Blanche once again had to drive back and forth to school, Rate decided that living in town had had its compensations after all.

First, there were the raw, cold, blustery winds of March. Since it had come in like a lamb, it was sure going out like a lion. The roads were a complete sea of mud. Ralph felt sorry for the poor horse picking his way through that cold, sloppy mess. It took a lot more time to clean a horse after they had been driven and splattered so with mud. All that caked dirt had to be cleaned off each evening, only to be equally as bad after a few yards on the road the next day.

Next came the April showers. Showers! Some of them were downright cloudbursts. Seemed like half the time, he and Blanche came home looking like something the cat dragged in—wet, mud-splattered, and not in the best of humor. 'Course, sometimes it was worth getting wet just to hear Blanche bellyache about her clothes getting sodden even though she had a blanket to cover her lap and legs. Sometimes, their coats had to be sponged off where another rig had splashed them, and then, Miney carefully tended them by the stove to have them dry by the next morning. Thinking of his mother, he guessed this kind of weather only added to her work too. Blanche tried to help, but Ma always said Blanche didn't do a good enough job. At least Blanche must have felt sorry for Ma too since she did the chicken chores to help Ma out a bit.

Rate guessed he'd be glad when school was done with for the summer. Besides, he'd heard talk that Elsie was going to build a new school this summer and that it was likely to have a basement and two stories. Sure would be different from the crowded wooden structure that served all eleven grades. The new building was to be built of brick and located just east of the present building. He supposed they'd start on it right after classes finished. Bet it was going to cost a tremendous amount of money.

The spring planting season was over. The winter wheat had survived the harsh winter weather well; the small field of oats looked good, and the corn was just beginning to peek through the ground, so the checkrows could be picked out here and there. Pa hadn't always checkrowed his corn, but he said this field would do better if it could be cultivated both ways to keep down the weeds. Rate knew it would mean less hoeing by him and the hired man, so he was all in favor of it. You see, when rows were checked, the hills of corn were the same distance apart from north to south as they were from east to west. Many farmers planted corn this way and used one horse on a single row cultivator to keep the weeds under control and to preserve the moisture for the corn.

*****

It was Monday morning, and at the breakfast table, Millie spoke to his young son.

"Rate, just got word that the sheepshearers will be here on Wednesday, so we'd best get the sheep washed today. I don't want you running off. I've got a few things to tend to, so I'll be ready about nine thirty or ten. Make sure you are within callin' distance."

"Yes, Pa."

This was the first year Pa had asked him to be around to help wash the sheep. Rate had known it was a job that needed doing since wool brought a better price if it wasn't so heavy with oil. He had asked Millie about this, and Millie told him he guessed the buyers would rather give a better price for clean wool and have the weight be all wool than to give less and have part of the weight be the sheep's natural body oil that had permeated the thick wool. Anyway, it made sense. Last year, he'd asked to go along, only Pa had told him he wasn't big enough. Rate hadn't figured to ask this year, so he was surprised and delighted with this new task delegated to him.

It was almost ten when Millie, Jim Keenan, and Ralph opened the gates to let the flock of seventy-five ewes out of the yard surrounding the sheep barn. One old ewe with a bell hanging on her collar, bellwether as they referred to her, was in the lead. Rate stood in the road to keep her from going south, and since she turned north, the rest of the flock automatically fell in behind. Sheep are notorious for following the leader; this was all well and good if the leader could be kept going in the right direction. The dust from the late June dryness rose in clouds as the sheep scurried on their way, darting here and there to nibble the lush, tender grass along the roadside.

Jim circled out into the fields to get by the flock because at the first corner north, the flock needed to turn east.

Rate chased a few stragglers out of the Garretts' front yard. When Ezz saw them coming, he had helped keep them from coming in around his buildings like any good neighbor would. Neighbors were always ready to lend a helping hand. Farmwork had to be a shared industry since it required so many hours of backbreaking hand labor. Some things were nigh impossible for a man to do by himself, and it wasn't every missus who was strong enough to be of assistance; besides, most farm men felt that fieldwork was not for women anyway. If she tended house and children, did the washin' and cookin' and bakin', tended garden and chickens, not to mention the sewing and patching, she had plenty of work of her own.

They made the turn east, and Jim kept the ewes from wandering into the Moores' or the Tabors'. By now, the old ewe settled down and acted as though she knew where she was going. Rate dashed to get ahead by the school to make sure she didn't turn south although he needn't have worried. She went north of her own accord, across the bridge spanning Maple River, and then turned east once more.

Not too much farther, there was a trail leading back to the river where a holding pen had been built across the river. They drove the sheep into the shallow water.

"Well, boy, get in there and start washing."

"Pants and all?"

Since it was summer, he wore no shoes, so no problem there.

"How else? Water's not very deep. Most likely won't come much over your knees."

Rate hardly relished the idea of wet pants even though they only came to his knees, so he quickly rolled his pant legs as high as they would go. The water, for all it was a warm June day, was still rather chilly. Rate watched his father and Jim wading amongst the sheep—they hadn't even bothered to roll up their pant legs—so he did likewise. They kneaded the wool on the sheep's back, pulling it up this way and that so it became saturated with water. Then, they moved on to the next.

Rate was busy at work and hadn't noticed that his father had come up behind him. The next thing he knew, he was bumped from behind, and down he went into the water, completely soaking his pants and the front half of his shirt.

"Oooops. Didn't know you was that close to me, boy. Guess you needn't have taken the time to roll up those pant legs. They look a little wet now."

"Pa, you did that on purpose," accused Ralph.

"Did what, Rate? Couldn't help it if I didn't know you was behind me, now could I?" Millie's chuckle rankled just a trifle.

"You could look around once in a while," suggested Rate.

"No harm's done, boy. You'll dry out by afternoon." Millie laughed.

Ralph knew his father had bumped him intentionally. Well, one of these days he'd get even.

When they were ready to leave, the bellwether took the lead once again, and the others obediently followed. They would be no trouble since all of them realized they were headed for home.

Rate, uncomfortable in his wet clothes, walked silently beside his father. Millie seemed to sense the lad was put out with him, so he became voluble.

"Several years ago, Rate, there was a man killed right where we were today. Seems he had a pretty good-sized ram in with his flock. He was squatted down, and for some reason, that ram lowered his head and charged. Before the man could get out of the way, the buck butted him right over the heart. Killed the man. Just like that. 'Course, don't think there's anything any harder than the head of a buck sheep. Just don't never pay not to keep an eye on them since no animal can always be trusted. It's usually the mild ones that do the damage 'cause farmers are notorious for not being cautious, get to havin' too much confidence in a well-mannered animal, and then bang! the animal goes wild, and the unwary farmer pays. Keep that in mind, boy, don't never put too much faith in a male animal, they can be awful treacherous."

Rate digested that bit of information. In later years, he was to say that never did he come by where the holding pens had once crossed the river without thinking of the unwary man who had lost his life there.

Wednesday, two men came to shear sheep. Ed Clark and Jim Keenan kept busy catching sheep to be sheared, one man did the shearing, while the second man kept a pair of sheep shears freshly sharpened. Millie was kept busy tying the wool in bundles.

A sheep bent on keeping its wool is not the easiest animal to handle. A body knew just how to grab the ewe, set her down between his legs, and commence. Around the ears and legs, it took some careful trimming. However, with shears razor-sharp, there was no need to open and close them along the belly, sides, and back; he could just keep them in an open position and slide the shears quickly down, neatly cutting a swath of wool close to the body. On occasion, he cut a little too close, usually around the head, and would nick a sheep. The red blood showed a sharp contrast to the glaring white coat of the newly sheared sheep. The bleats chorused a cacophony of sound as the frightened sheep cried out their despair. However, as soon as they were released to join their newly shorn companions, they became once more at ease and didn't seem to mind that they had just lost their heavy winter coat. How white they looked! Rate always felt that they looked completely naked until the snow-white wool began to get darkened with oil and dirt once again.

A couple of days after the sheep had been sheared, Millie loaded the bundles of wool on the wagon to take in to H. J. Hankins to sell. There was over 250 pounds of wool, and he was paid nineteen cents a pound, thus getting almost fifty dollars. Millie felt this was a fairly good price and was well pleased with the amount, figuring he'd had a good return for the work involved.

Fact was, things were going pretty darned good this year. Prices had held steadier than normal. The first of June, he had sold Hankins over sixteen tons of hay at a price of $6.75 a ton. Since he hadn't been feeding so many hogs over the winter, he'd had a goodly quantity of corn left over, so he'd sold some at fifty-five cents a bushel, and he'd had extra oats, which he'd sold for forty-two and a half cents a bushel.

He still had some of both commodities left just in case he didn't get a crop this year. However, the corn was off to a good start, and the oats looked good. Still, Millie always said a bird in the hand was worth two in the bush—he knew just how quickly adverse weather conditions could ruin the prospects of a good harvest. He had long ago learned that the old saying of "don't count your chickens before they're hatched" sure applied to a good-looking crop in the field. Frost before corn was ripe, heavy rain at harvest, which knocked the wheat and oats flat or perhaps sprouted them while they stood in the shock—these were always an ever-present threat to the farmer.

Millie had just always accepted whatever came as being something he couldn't control, and since he couldn't control it, there was no sense to worry about it. If things went wrong this year, likely next year would be better. Besides, Miney worried enough for the both of them—that was one reason he figured she was always so close with money; she was always afraid there wouldn't be any more coming, so she pinched her pennies and stretched a dollar until it hollered. He laughed as he thought of it. 'Course Miney was a right fine wife, and he liked her just the way she was.

Miney came flouncing into the house, banging the screen door.

Millie looked up expectantly from the paper he was reading, an amused expression on his face.

"And who's always yellin' at Rate 'bout slammin' doors?"

"I just don't care. That George Schenck makes me furious."

"What's he done now?"

"Remember last week when I told you he saw me coming out of the house to mail a letter, and even though I hollered and waved at him to stop, he just drove right off? Now, this time is even worse."

"What's worse?"

"See this?" She waved a piece of paper in the air. "Well, it's a note he left along with the letter he never took. You see, I didn't have any stamps, so I put my letter in the mailbox along with two pennies to cover the cost of a stamp. Well, sir, just listen to what he wrote. 'Lick your own stamps!' Now, doesn't that beat all? He left the letter, took my money, and left a stamp." She showed the letter and stamp. "Just you wait until I see that man. I'll give him a piece of my mind."

Millie started to laugh.

"I don't see why you think it's so funny. I did want this letter to go out today. Isn't it part of his job?"

"Don't think it says anywhere whether he has to lick stamps for his patrons or not."

"Always knew when we were in school together that he was lazy and irresponsible. How'd he ever get to be a mail carrier anyway?"

"Now, Miney, don't make such a big thing of it. Just learn to buy more than one stamp at a time, and then you won't be likely to have that problem."

Miney moved off to the kitchen muttering to herself.

Ralph had listened to the verbal exchange. Frankly, he thought the note was comical. Somehow, Ma was always late going anyplace, and even though she knew Mr. Schenck was always here so regular you could set your clock by him, she always waited until the last minute to go to the mailbox. She just hated to buy more than one stamp at a time, so she was always running out. Mr. Schenck had tolerated this a few times. Must be he'd just plain got tired of Ma putting the money in the box. Bet from now on, Ma would stamp her own letters even if it did rankle a mite. Of course, if she did meet Mr. Schenck up town, she'd give him a tongue- lashing even if it wouldn't do any good. From what everyone said, Mr. Schenck could be an ornery cuss. Ma just needed to have a better sense of humor at times. Now, Pa had seen the funny side of it too. 'Course the note almost sounded like something Pa would say, so that was probably why it tickled him.

When Millie had purchased his farm from his father, there had been two tracts of eighty acres of land, so it had extended as far north as the next road. However, after a short period of time, he felt this was an excessive burden of debt, so he had sold the north eighty to his brother John. Now, being the trader he was, John had no sooner acquired the property when he traded it back to Horatio in exchange for a farm north of Elsie. This had left Millie with the south eighty and Horatio once again in possession of the north eighty.

A portion of the north eighty had been cleared of timber, the stumps burned out, and the fields had been plowed a few years before these transactions. Horatio had approached his son about the advisability of continuing to farm the fields rather than let them lay idle. Whether Horatio actually hinted that if Millie worked the place on shares, it would someday be his is rather doubtful. However, Millie assumed that this was the agreement. Of course, nothing was put in writing, and at this time, neither Horatio nor Millie realized this was to be the genesis of a quarrel.

Millie was glad of the extra land for crops since most of his own land back of the ditch had only been used for pasture, and stumps still dotted the terrain. Often on a Sunday afternoon, Rate would accompany his father to these back fields while Milford set fire to a stump or two. The sheep kept the vegetation nibbled so short all around the stumps, there was little danger of the fire spreading. Sometimes a stump would smolder underground a day or two with small wisps of smoke rising intermittently above the blackened hole, a silent indicator that the fire was still feeding on the roots of the once forest giant.

This year, like last, the field across from the Garretts had been a hayfield. Several days of rain the first part of July delayed the final putting up of the hay from this particular field, which was the last one Millie had. Then, came two days that were beautifully bright and sunny and hot, ideal haying weather. The hay had been cut, raked, and was now standing in the haycocks, waiting for someone to load and haul it.

Millie, Jim, Merval, and Ralph were getting ready to do that very thing.

A few days ago, Millie had traded off Mage to Cash Waldron for a younger mare. Rate hadn't been sorry to see Mage go since the boy had never forgiven the horse for standing on his foot. Besides, Mage hadn't learned from the episode, and the only thing that kept there from being a recurrence was that Ralph had learned to be extremely careful when in the stall alongside Mage. He paid particular attention to how close he got to the horse's feet and was prepared to move his own in a hurry. Anyway, the new mare hadn't been hitched up with any of Millie's horses since the acquisition. Millie decided the hay wagon was a good time to try her out, so they harnessed her in with Cap.

All went well. Rate drove the team while Merval and Jim pitched the hay from the cocks onto the wagon and Millie made the load. When Millie decided they had put on a good enough load, Jim took the lines to take the team into the road and home.

There was a slight incline to go up before they reached the road. When spoken to, Cap stepped into the collar to pull, but Dolly hung back; when Cap stepped back, she surged forward. Poor Cap didn't know what to do. He tried again, and as soon as his tugs tightened, Dolly stepped back. She began to prance, she tried to turn sideways, she even tried to rear. Jim, who was uncommonly good with a team, could do nothing with her.

There was a small sapling growing in the fenceline a few yards off, so Millie stepped over to this and cut it off with his jackknife. He took the lines from Jim and told the others to stand back; he stood off to one side, the lines firmly grasped in one large hand, the sapling in the other.

Millie spoke, his voice deep and powerful, "Get up there."

Dolly didn't even make an effort.

Millie raised the sapling and struck her rump a resounding blow; she neighed and pranced, but didn't attempt to pull. Again a blow fell with much the same results. Poor Cap danced and pranced and didn't know for certain what was expected of him.

By now, Millie was fast losing his patience. He began to rain blows methodically and with vigor while a string of profanity came forth, the likes of which Rate had never heard. To be sure, he sometimes heard Millie swear, but nothing that held a candle to this. He fairly stared at his father. What if Ma had heard? His mother was not one to condone taking the Lord's name in vain, and yet here was Pa spewing out blasphemous words with gusto.

Millie stopped as suddenly as he had begun. He tossed the sapling aside; it looked a little worse for wear, no leaves, and the bark hung in shreds. His voice took on a new tone as he spoke soothingly to the team. Cap quieted, but every muscle along Dolly's ribs and flank quivered with anticipation, and her eyes rolled white in fright.

"Cap. Dolly. Get up there," spoke Millie firmly.

There was no hesitation this time. Both horses surged forward as a team should, and the wagon creaked into the road.

"Whoa!"

The team stopped. Sweat was running off Dolly as she awaited the next command.

"Jim, you get back up there and see if she don't drive all right now," ordered Millie.

There was no further confrontation. Dolly did not balk again that day; her decorum was perfect in every way.

Several days later, Jim was once again driving Dolly when she refused the command to go. Millie didn't even bother to pick up the lines. He merely shouted from some distance away, "Dolly, you sonofabitch, get up there." Dolly obediently did as she was told.

Rate figured he had learned at least one thing. He hadn't liked seeing Dolly beaten, and Pa had sure dressed her out good, but he did understand that horses had to be taught to mind if they were to be of service. A horse that balked every now and then was not much use to a farmer. He hoped he would never have to take such drastic measures because he didn't like hurting an animal. 'Course, he remembered that Pa hadn't struck any too lightly when giving him a whipping, so he guessed a horse, being so much bigger, could tolerate a lot more.

*****

"Millie, I'd like a few extra dollars to buy some material for aprons, and I do need a couple of new housedresses. I thought since you just sold some hay and grain, now would be a good time to get what I need."

Milford's face took on an uncommunicative expression. "Perhaps you'd best wait until I sell those yearlings."

"Why on earth do I have to wait? You said it would be a month or more before you sold them."

"I'm a little short of cash right now," he hedged.

"Short of cash? You can't be. There haven't been that many expenses, and I know you've been getting a good price for what you've sold. Don't you want me to have the money?"

"It's not that, Miney."

"Well then, what is it? I don't usually ask for much."

He knew by the tone of her voice that her feelings had been hurt, and he hadn't intended to do that.

"I know you don't ask for much. I never complain, do I?"

"No, but you've never refused me before."

Millie heaved a sigh.

"I honestly don't have the cash because I bought a flock of a hundred sheep from Pa."

"Sheep? Why do we need more sheep, and how'd your father get a flock anyhow?"

"He had loaned a man some money and taken a mortgage on the flock. Well, the man couldn't pay, and Pa had to foreclose. Anyway, they aren't far from here, so he gave me first chance to buy them."

"For a good price, I'll bet."

"Pa only asked $210 for the whole lot. That's what the note was for. He didn't even make any to cover his trouble."

"$210! Good heavens, Millie, since when are sheep worth that much? I thought you just sold one for $1.50."

"I did, but she was an ewe that hadn't got bred, so I sold her cheap. No, Miney, I'm sure they are worth that much."

"You'd think they were just because that is the price your father set on them. I honestly don't understand you even a little bit. You think your father knows all there is to know, and, Milford, I don't always trust your father when it comes to business. I still remember how he took Pa on trading horses."

"Let's not dredge that up. Pa's always been fair with me. He just thought I'd stand to make a tidy sum on these sheep."

"I know, and you're still willing to let your father do your thinking for you," she said bitterly.

"Now, Miney, that's not fair. As soon as I get some extree cash, I'll see that you have whatever you need."

From the tone of his voice, Miney knew the matter was settled. Sometimes he did try her patience. She had thought when Father and Mother Setterington moved to South Lyon, Millie would be free to be his own man, but she had been wrong. Millie was still like a puppet on a string where his father was concerned. Of course, in all fairness, she had to admit that there were times when Father had helped Millie to invest money and, in a short time, make a sizable amount on his investment.

She was certain it had been on his father's advice that Millie and Mr. Curtis had bought a couple of houses in Elsie—one for taxes and one was estate property. They had fixed the houses up a bit, new paint and paper, and made a few minor repairs. They'd sold the one house for a tidy profit and had been renting the other one, which made a steady income, although when it was divided in half, it wasn't very much. Of course, just the fact that they could count on that rent money each month made it worthwhile.

She honestly doubted if Millie would have had the courage to attempt something like that without his father standing behind him, prodding him along. Father Setterington had just the right amount of gambling spirit to make him dare to speculate. Millie wanted to invest only in a sure thing. Perhaps some of this was her influence because she simply hated putting money out when they might not get it back. Still, Father did seem to get his back, and he usually got a generous profit. Why, she'd heard that as far back as in the 1880s, he had charged 10 percent interest. She didn't even dare guess what he charged now. No getting around it, Father knew how to make money. 'Course, he never let his emotions enter into a business deal. No, sir, there were times when he was coldly calculating, and a person would have thought he had ice in his veins.

She supposed she'd just have to wait for her material. It did rankle a bit because Millie never discussed anything with her— just went ahead and did as he pleased, or rather what his father pleased. Well, she'd just keep close track, and as soon as he sold something, she'd be sure she got her money, and just maybe she'd buy some material for a good dress even though she had thought she'd make do until fall.

The summer was passing quickly. Haying season was finished, and it was time to harvest wheat. Next, the oats would be turning, and then there would be only a short time left of summer vacation. Rate and Curly were enjoying being together again. They often went over to Maple River back of the Pages' and fished. Sometimes, they had good luck, sometimes not. If Rate was lucky, Ma could have fish for a whole meal. If not, she always cooked what he caught just for him. Yup, in ways like that, Ma was awful good to him, and she never complained about doin' it neither.

When the boys were back to the river, they often saw blacksnakes slither into the water only a few feet away from where they walked along the bank. Some of these snakes were six feet long and almost as large around as Ralph's wrist. The boys had no fear of them since the snakes made every effort to get away from them as quickly as possible. In fact, they liked to watch the snakes swim effortlessly in the water.

Mostly, they fished from the trunk of a tree that had become uprooted and had fallen into the water. This made a good place to sit, and there was no need for long poles. Besides, neither of them had a proper store- bought fishing pole, they had simply cut themselves a hefty willow from along the roadside, trimmed off the leaves and small branches, and tied a piece of string to the end. A washer served as a sinker, a used cork from a bottle as a bobber, and sometimes a bent pin had to suffice as a hook. Both boys wore straw hats pushed back on their heads; while Rate had a white, unblemished complexion, the bridge of Don's nose and his cheeks were peppered with freckles, giving him an impish look. For boys who sometimes found it difficult to remain quiet for very long while in school, they could sit on that old tree trunk for hours, seldom talking because they didn't want to scare the fish. Their legs and feet were deeply tanned from sitting so long in the sun. Their arms were tanned as far as the rolled-up shirtsleeves allowed. They seldom argued, although neither was above playing a prank on the other now and then, and they often wrestled for the fun of it.

They became inseparable, seeming to want to cram a whole lifetime of living into these few brief summer months. Miney had even let the two of them sleep in the haymow one night when Don had slept over with Rate. It was at the end of haying season, and both boys had looked so enthusiastic about the idea, she hadn't had the heart to refuse. Newly mowed hay had a pleasant odor, so perhaps she could understand their desire just a little. Besides, she knew if Millie had got wind of the request, he would have overridden any negative decision of hers. In some things, Millie was quick to side in with Ralph—unless it in some way affected Blanche.

Blanche was watching out the south window, her eyes following a man leading a cow along the road toward their place. As he drew nearer, she recognized him as Monroe Swarthout from up on the corner. Out of idle curiosity, she moved to yet another window so she could watch the man's progress. The man turned into their driveway and, after some problem at the gate, took the cow into the barnyard.

Blanche wondered what was going on. This was not the first time this had happened. A week or so ago, it had been Roy Brown, a few days ago, John Fizzell, and now Mr. Swarthout.

Then, she remembered that one afternoon she had been the only one home when Mr. Brown had come by. He had seemed rather embarrassed when he found out her father wasn't at home. He'd dug a work-dirty hand into his overalls and come out with a folded piece of money; he'd smoothed it out and given her the dollar saying he owed it to her father. When she had asked what it was for, he'd only become more embarrassed and had even got red around the ears. He'd hung his head and said, "For a service last week an' the week afore thet. He'll know." Then, before she could say anything more, he'd taken off like a burnt boot, and she'd been left there holding the money.

When she'd given her father the money, he'd just nodded and said it was to settle an account.

Blanche hated being treated like a child. So today, feeling in a particularly spunky mood, she descended on her unwary mother in the kitchen.

"Ma, why's Mr. Swarthout bringing a cow here?"

Miney looked around at her daughter, the expression on her face showing how completely taken aback she was by the suddenness of the question.

"Why, why," she stammered, "I didn't know he had."

"I just watched him come through the gate. Mr. Brown and Mr. Fizzell have brought cows too. What's going on? They always take them back home, so I know Pa's not buying their cows."

"They...well, they bring them to visit our cows."

"What for? Seems like a dumb idea to me."

"Well, that's what they do. They come for a visit," she stated emphatically, then added in a more modified voice, "When you're older, you'll understand better."

"Understand what? If you don't explain anything, there's nothing for me to understand. Well, if you won't tell me, I'll just ask Pa when he comes in for dinner."

With that declaration, Blanche made a hurried exit.

Goodness, Blanche obviously meant what she said. Miney had no idea what kind of an answer Millie would give the girl. It was such a delicate situation. If only Blanche hadn't been quite so observant.

True to her word, Blanche put the question to her father. He gave her a long expressionless look, then said, "They bring them here to be serviced."

The tone of the answer told Blanche she was not to ask any more questions. Now, she was more perplexed than ever.

That night, after she and Ralph had gone upstairs to bed, she sneaked into his room and sat on the edge of his bed. Rate looked at her wonderingly. It wasn't often his sister did this, only if something was bothering her.

"Ralph, do you know why the neighbors bring those cows here?"

"Sorta," he said hesitantly.

"Tell me," she demanded.

"They take 'em in where Pa keeps the bull. Pa hasn't never let me go along, but I peeked through a crack once, and I could hear them talking. Whatever they do had to be done if the cow is to have a calf."

"Oh."

Blanche had known that cows had calves, mares had foals, sows had pigs, because there were some things that farm children just grew up with and accepted as the normal course of events. However, no one ever quite got around to telling them why the animals gave birth; this was something to be ignored—the fact that a female had to have mated with a male.

"Ralph, do you suppose that is why we keep a ram with the sheep?" she asked wonderingly.

"Guess I'd never given it much mind. Could likely be. Everyone I know who keeps sheep keeps a ram, or they sometimes lease one for a short time."

"Thanks, Ralph. Now, go to sleep."

Blanche returned to her bedroom more puzzled than ever. There were so many questions she would like to ask, but Ma just never was one to explain anything. Sometimes, she felt Ma hated to admit there were male and female anything.

Not all farmers kept a bull on their farm, especially if they only kept three or four milch cows. Millie had let it be known that he had a good- looking Holstein, and those who brought a cow to be serviced paid fifty cents. It had turned out to be quite profitable. Millie also found that he could command a much better price for a bred heifer than one that was open, so the bull was surely paying his way and then some.

Once again, come the latter part of October, the Setteringtons moved back into Grandma Smith's house. It wasn't all that bad. In fact, Ralph was glad to see some of his friends again. Guess maybe he had the best of two worlds—the farm in the summer when it was really the most pleasant place to be, and town in the winter when the weather was bad.

Yes, the summers were really pleasant. Rate enjoyed doing any fieldwork, which involved driving a horse. Now, the hoeing was something he could do without, but it could have been worse. He liked working with the animals. Sometimes, it took a heap o' doin' to outsmart them.

Winter work wasn't anything to enjoy. The ice froze in the tank, and a hole had to be chopped so the livestock could get a drink. Then, when the water had to be pumped by hand, he stood there half frozen, methodically moving the pump handle up and down while his nose lost its feeling and his fingers felt numb. He also remembered the time he had stuck his tongue on the pump handle and had been completely surprised to learn that it stuck there. When he pulled it away, he left a small patch of skin on the iron handle. At dinner, when he hadn't eaten very much because of his sore tongue, Millie chuckled like it was something extraordinarily comical. Then, he explained, "Rate, I'd bet my bottom dollar that in town, every kid at some time or other sticks his tongue on a hitching post, and every farm lad tries a pump handle—all with the same result. Guess you won't never do it again, will you?"

Rate had been emphatic in stating he had learned his lesson. Pa's words had made him feel better even if Pa had laughed since he realized now that he wasn't the only dummy in the world. The next generation of boys was to learn on ice skate keys—they were such a handy size to pop in the mouth with the same results.

Since the horses stood in the stable all the time, there was a lot of manure to fork out daily; they had to be bedded down extra good to try to keep their stable blankets as clean as possible. In fact, it took a lot of time to pull straw from the stack behind the barn and carry it into the stable. He'd get a really big forkful, with the straw hanging together well, then just before he got into the stable, it would have loosened enough, so half of it fell off. Sometimes, it was enough to make him swear even though he knew Ma didn't approve of swearing.

True, he still had horses to care for in town, but usually there were only two instead of six or eight. Usually at night, a group would go sledding or skating. Sometimes, the older ones went on class sleigh rides. Well, a couple more years, and he'd be old enough for that.

'Course, it really didn't matter whether he liked the present arrangement or not, Blanche was the only one who counted. In all fairness, he did realize that during the heaviest part of the winter, it would not have been all that pleasant for Blanche to drive to school, yet other girls did it. Of course, they weren't the only daughter of Milford and Mina Setterington. Wonder why the only son never seemed to matter?

Rate was well pleased with the new school building. It was a huge, two-storied, red brick building with cut stones set in at the corners for design. The gray slate roof sloped sharply upward, making the edifice look taller than it actually was. The front of the school faced east where the arched, stone-decorated entrance shielded the double doors leading upstairs to the classrooms. The new building had been built in front of the old two-storied wooden structure that had since been sold and moved away.

Even the belfry held a brand-new bell, the old one being considered too small for the growing community. The building looked naked standing there with no bushes to make it appear part of the landscape; it was stark, and bare, and its newness made it stand out like a sore thumb. 'Course, once a person got inside, all this was forgotten, and if the outside had an austere look, like it didn't yet belong, the rooms were pleasant, and the teachers gloried in the new space and improved facilities.

Since Ralph was now in the fifth grade, his classroom was on the main floor. However, he had gone upstairs where the high school students had their classes and had even been on an excursion to the basement just to look things over. He noted the classrooms were light, airy, and spacious after the cramped quarters of the old building.

Blanche had long ago decided she liked town best. She was not one to care for the smells often emanating from a farm. She could do without the smell of freshly spread manure in a field, the stink of the hogpens, the stuffiness of the chicken coop when she went to gather eggs. The flies were not nearly as bad in town, and she certainly didn't miss carting milk to Doyle's cheese factory and smelling the stink from that, not to mention the smell of the whey they took home for the pigs.

Besides, she had friends in town, and they always had something to do. They often met at each other's house and sometimes did their homework together. Often, on the farm, she was lonely, lacking someone her own age to talk to. She had never been close to the Swarthout girls or Selina Clark, who were her nearest neighbors. Farm girls had a different outlook on life and accepted not having money much of the time. Blanche had seen too much of the comforts money could buy to be content living a meager existence on a farm like some folks did.

Miney felt it was easier living in town. She didn't have chickens to take care of, and she no longer had the milk can to wash since Millie took care of that. She could send Ralph to the store every day instead of having to wait until Saturday to buy groceries. She had to admit that on the days when she sent him to the store before school, at dinnertime, and after school, he sometimes seemed a little resentful. Well, she tried not to make him go before school, but there were times when it was a dire necessity. She knew exactly how much each item cost and carefully doled out the money. Often Ralph was sent for exactly one pound of beefsteak, cut thin, and since it was twelve cents a pound, twelve cents was all Miney gave him. She expected the butcher to be that accurate with his cutting.

Besides, Miney had grown up in town, and she liked having neighbors next door. Lorin lived just down the street, and while there was a great difference in their ages, she and her half sister did get on well. Lorin did a lot of knitting, so she often brought her knitting and spent the afternoon with Miney. Miney always had something she was crocheting, or sometimes in the winter, she worked on braiding a rug. For this, she used heavy wool material from old coats or trousers, cutting the material in narrow strips, then deftly turning under the raw edges as she put the three strands into a braid. The extra warmth of the material on her lap was a welcome feature when the winter winds howled and the curtains moved lazily back and forth because nothing fit snugly, and the cold air sneaked through each and every crack.

At the back of the house was a large attached woodshed, so one didn't have to go outdoors to bring in kindling. At the farm, Ralph had had to keep kindling piled by the door, but it was often snow-covered and somewhat damp to put in the stove. This was much better.

Then, too, she was within walking distance of church. Miney always dreaded getting a horse around in the winter. The horse had to be blanketed when they stopped, and it was such a nuisance getting the blanket on and off. She was always just a little afraid of tipping the cutter over when they had to go through uneven drifts, and sometimes there were drifts as high as the horse's belly. Of course, the menfolk often did some shoveling in these spots, and the thills of the cutter were off-set so the horse could travel in the tracks of a team rather than having to break new snow. Still, when all was added up, the convenience of being in town was greater than the pleasures of the farm. Perhaps one of the greatest plus factors was that Miney realized it made life easier and more pleasant for her daughter.

Millie knew without a doubt that both Blanche and Miney liked living in town. Although it made more work for him having to drive to the farm twice each day, he really didn't mind all that much. However, he had been giving considerable thought to the farming situation. He liked the work well enough and had been making a comfortable living, but he knew he would never acquire the wealth his father had. Perhaps he could do better if he owned a business. Pa had been lucky to have had his father help him get started. Millie didn't like bookwork all that much, and being in the banking business held no fascination for him, but there must be something he could do. He had a little money saved, so perhaps he should keep watch for someone wanting to sell his business. Millie felt there were several things he could adequately handle. A general store couldn't be all that difficult, a livery stable, or perhaps a butcher shop. Well, it was food for thought. He wondered if Pa would think some sort of business was a step in the right direction.

Whether Milford decided he liked living in town better, or whether he felt it kept his womenfolk happier, or if he simply wanted to emulate his father, that next summer, he decided that come fall, they would move to town for good. He had found someone to rent the farm on shares, and he had the offer to sell farm implements for Roy Pierce's dad. Besides, he could still trade horses and supplement his income there. He intended to keep his flock of sheep on the south forty and would bring them back to the eighty for the winter months and lambing time. He had meticulously worked this out with the renter and had had papers drawn up so each knew what to expect; there was the division of the wheat Millie had planted in the fall to be harvested by the renter. The renter was also to take responsibility for doing Millie's roadwork.

Each year the farmers took turns grading, hauling gravel, or perhaps improving a ditch alongside the road; an elected roadmaster was the one who assigned the duties for a given area, and this now became the duty of the renter.

In the fall of 1904, the Setteringtons moved bag and baggage into Elsie. Before, they had never moved any of their own furniture, they simply had used Grandma Smith's. Now, they moved some of Grandma's to the attic, sold some, and added the rest to their own—that which was kept included four chairs with cane bottoms, which had been made by Miney's grandfather Barnes and a rocking chair that Miney's mother had brought from New York State. Miney had been quite upset on moving day when the glass on the secretary had been cracked. Well, she guessed she was lucky it hadn't been completely broke out; she could live with it only being cracked near the bottom of the door.

Ralph couldn't dispel a feeling of sadness as he settled down to permanent town life. He had liked the farm, he liked the animals, he even liked what little bit of fieldwork he was allowed to do. Chores weren't all that bad either—they were just like anything else, they had their bad moments when the weather wasn't good.

He enjoyed hearing the whip-poor-wills call, and often the silence of the night was broken by the cry of a screech owl. Some people hated hearing them because folks said a screech owl foreboded death. Ma said this wasn't rightly so, and he believed her. Besides, how could one of those cute little bundle of feathers have anything to do with people dying? Just like some folks were scared when a dog howled at a full moon—said the dog did this because they smelled death in the air. Rate didn't believe this either. Folks always had to come up with an explanation for everything, and some of the explanations were pretty far-fetched.

Often a barn owl or two lived in one of the outbuildings, and Rate liked to watch the sleepy-eyed bird sitting oblivious to anything going on during the day. Then, too, in town, one seldom saw the hawks sailing in the sky. He knew that chicken hawks sometimes helped themselves to a meal of baby chicks, and he'd seen his father grab his shotgun and shoot more than one of these predators as they hovered, ready to plummet down on an unwary chick. After one such occurrence, the chicks went into a frenzy every time a shadow passed overhead. Anyway, there were other kinds of hawks who ate only rodents, and he loved to see them sailing the wind currents, their wings outspread and motionless, a true spectacle of beauty.

In town, there sure weren't going to be the woodchucks, not to mention seeing the muskrats along the river or ditch or swampy areas. Living in town all year long was sure going to be a lot different.

He wondered just what he would find to do to occupy himself come summer when school was out. During the winter, there was ice-skating or sledding right after school, then hurry home to get chores done before it was time to eat; there was no going out again after supper, but there were lessons to be done and books to be read, so he didn't have all that much free time. They even had a library at school now. It didn't have many books as yet, but he had brought a few home. He always looked forward to getting books for Christmas; besides, if a book was really good, he didn't mind reading it two or three times.

Oh, well, summer was a long ways off, no use giving it too much thought now.

This is the secretary with the broken glass. It is still in the family.

Ralph on the South 40 acres.

One of Ralph's favorite horses.

www.ingramcontent.com/pod-product-compliance
Lightning Source LLC
Chambersburg PA
CBHW021627120626
46545CB00002B/432